DEAN R. ESSLINGER

Immigrants and the City

Ethnicity and Mobility in a Nineteenth-Century Midwestern Community

National University Publications
KENNIKAT PRESS • 1975
Port Washington, N.Y. • London

Manufactured in the United States of America

Published by
Kennikat Press Corp.
Port Washington, N.Y. / London

Library of Congress Cataloging in Publication Data

Esslinger, Dean R
    Immigrants and the city.

    (Interdisciplinary urban studies) (National uni-
versity publications)
    Bibliography: p.
    Includes index.
    1. South Bend, Ind.—Foreign population. 2. Ur-
banization—South Bend, Ind. 3. Social mobility—
South Bend, Ind. I. Title.
F534.S7E77   301.32'9'77289   75-15947
ISBN 0-8046-9108-8

CONTENTS

TABLES

MAPS

PREFACE

This study of ethnic mobility on the midwestern urban frontier grew out of an enquiry that began in late 1967. My concern then was to use the manuscript federal census to examine the relation between immigration and urban growth in a single city. By combining the traditional methods of historical research with the newer techniques of quantitative analysis I expected to learn more about the urban process as it affected and was affected by the lives of thousands of immigrants. The data from the census records provided the necessary information about jobs, ages, places of birth, or property. Newspapers, biographies, local histories, and city directories supplemented the basic census data and gave hints of the flavor of life in a changing urban environment. Labeled now as the "new urban history," this approach seemed the most objective and precise way of studying social history "from the bottom up."

The manuscript federal census has always offered a wealth of information to historians, but the problem until recently was how to analyze so much data about thousands of persons. The development, however, of a fairly sophisticated quantitative methodology aided by the use of a computer has solved much of that problem. By keypunching the census data onto computer cards it is possible to find out not only the occupational or age patterns of ethnic groups, but also to trace the changes that occurred in the status of thousands of specific individuals over a period of time. Studies of migration and social mobility can be made without having to rely on the evidence from only a few "representative" cases.

One limitation of the manuscript federal census is that there are so few years for which the records are detailed enough and available. Before 1850 the census did not record information on specific individuals by name. After 1880 the federal records are not available because of the fire which destroyed them (for 1890) and the laws which have kept those since 1900 closed to the public. Therefore the census information can be most effectively used to study immigration and urbanization in a city that experienced rapid growth and change between 1850 and 1880. South Bend, Indiana, is such a city.

In 1850, when the census takers probably knew nearly everyone in South Bend, they recorded the names of the individuals in each household along with their occupation, age, sex, color, value of real estate owned, whether they were married or attended school within the last year, and whether they were illiterate or had handicaps. In subsequent census years more questions were asked, including the value of personal property (1860), whether or not an individual's parents were foreign-born (1870), and the parents' place of birth (1880).

Although the historian might wish for even more information, a major part of the frustration in using the census records comes not from the lack of data, but from the internal inconsistencies, ambiguities, and inaccuracies of the records. In a study of mobility, in which individuals are traced from census to census, it can be maddening to find misspellings, Anglicized names, or phonetic spellings. Thus the wife of an easily identifiable businessman appears as "Lucetta" in 1860, as "Lisette" in 1870, and as "Lozetta" in 1880. The historian is also faced with determining through city directories and other sources what distinctions the census taker had in mind when he labeled one immigrant a "furniture maker" and another a "furniture manufacturer."

Inaccuracies in the reporting of age and wealth have discouraged many users of the manuscript federal census.[1] As South Bend grew in population, it sometimes took from June to November to complete the census count—long enough to allow much movement to take place, ages to change, and errors to occur. Moreover, the historian should never forget the human frailties of the census takers themselves. There may have been truth as well as humor in the lament by a local booster that the census count was less than expected because the "marshal is fat and short of breath and the summer was very hot."[2]

If the historian, knowing the limitations and pitfalls of relying on census information, has either the nerve or naïveté to proceed, he is faced with the problem of how to analyze thousands of facts efficiently and objectively. The validity of the conclusions to be drawn depends heavily upon the questions that are asked. As Professors Marshall Smelser and William Davison, two of the early supporters of this project, have said, "After all, what is a collection of historical data but a collection of answers waiting to be questioned?"[3] Some questions have already been asked and are available for application in the form of canned computer programs. The development of computer programs and techniques for analyzing quantitative historical data is progressing rapidly, and the best advice for the novice is to keep a sharp eye on such journals as the *Historical Methods Newsletter*.

For this study I decided to use all persons recorded in the census for South Bend who were either foreign-born or whose parents were foreign-born. This resulted in the examination of facts on over 10,000 cases—a quantity still manageable for a single historian with modest means at his disposal and some degree of patience. Because all the available immigrants and their children were used, many of the difficulties of a random sampling system were avoided. Such thoroughness, however, is a luxury one could not afford in studies of larger cities like Boston or Omaha.

Once the information had been sorted through the computer and various cross-tabulations were performed (such as counting the number of workers in each occupation from each foreign country according to the city ward they were living in), the most exciting part of the research began. The analysis of the results from scores of questions began to reveal the rough framework of the life patterns of immigrant families in a growing midwestern city. As the quantitative information from the census on occupations, property, age, education, residence, persistence, and ethnicity was collated and then supplemented with information from other sources, the relation between urbanization and immigration in nineteenth-century South Bend became more distinctly visible.

It is appropriate at the completion of a project such as this to thank those who gave willingly of their time and thoughts. The largest share of my gratitude goes to Professor John A. Williams, who guided the study chapter by chapter. I am also indebted to Professor Philip Gleason, who has been a teacher, friend, and generous critic. Others who read the manuscript and gave helpful suggestions were Professors Jay C. Dolan and George Friedman. From Stephan Thernstrom, whose writings first stirred my interest in the study of urban mobility, I received valuable advice. The Social Science Training and Research Laboratory of the University of Notre Dame provided an important measure of financial and technical assistance without which the analysis of thousands of census records would have been impossible. Professor William I. Davison, in particular, encouraged me in the technical problems that the study produced. Mrs. Hugh Edsall of the South Bend Public Library and Miss Martha Merrill of the Northern Indiana Historical Society were genial hosts who made much of the research a pleasant experience. My deepest thanks, however, is to my wife, Sandy, who has been patient and loving in her encouragement. It is to her and our children, Regina, Joel, and Carey, that this book is dedicated.

IMMIGRANTS AND THE CITY

1

INTRODUCTION

For many Americans living in the last half of the nineteenth century the pattern of life was shaped by two common experiences: urbanization and immigration. Together with the rapid growth of industry these forces transformed America, and the movement of large numbers of immigrants into the cities resulted in dramatic changes in the economic and occupational structure as well as in such fundamental social institutions as the church and the family. For a majority of immigrants these changes were all part of a single experience: movement across the Atlantic was also a move into an urbanized, industrial society. Perhaps even more significant than the movement to the frontier, this movement of populations into the cities was the force that shaped and controlled American society after the Civil War.

But despite the fact that historians have long been aware of the significance of urbanization and immigration in our national history, there has been only a limited effort to find out how these two factors have been related to each other. There are of course many good studies which analyze immigrant populations in an urban setting. General works such as Rowland Berthoff's *British Immigrants in Industrial America, 1790–1950,* or Carl Wittke's *We Who Built America* contain valuable information and comments on the distribution and settlement of immigrants in urban centers. None of these studies, however, deliberately examines the role immigrants had in the urbanization of the nation. The urban setting is incidental to their primary purpose, describing and analyzing the arrival and eventual adjustment of the foreign-born to the American environment.[1]

The historians of the foreign-born have not sufficiently explored the role of the immigrant in the growth of cities, but the urban historians have not satisfactorily examined the problem either. Perhaps this is largely due to ignorance of the histories of various cities or even disagreement as to what is meant by *urbanization*. Arthur Schlesinger alerted historians to the significance of the rise of the city in 1933, but historians have not agreed on how this growth should be studied. Some urban historians like Richard Wade, Constance McLaughlin Green, Bessie Pierce, and Bayrd Still have followed the pattern first set by Schlesinger, studying specific cities or specific problems within the context of well-established themes in the nation's history.[2] Other works in urban history have concentrated on special problems of the physical structure and growth of the cities or on the importance of the city as an idea or image.[3] Although these historians add to the understanding of the city, they vary widely in their conception of what the essential elements of the urbanization process are or what the proper method to be used in studying urban history is. In part this has been the fault of pioneers like Schlesinger, who called attention to the importance of the urban movement but did not provide historians with a clear definition of the process of urban growth.

Left to find their own framework for urban history, some recent historians have become more aware of the findings and methods of the social sciences.[4] In part this emphasis upon the social sciences is caused by the increasing awareness that urbanization as a process can best be understood by studying the composition of populations and their distribution in time and space. As Dwight Hoover has suggested, "The theoretical

framework for the urban historian . . . should be the study of
population change. The necessary social data is to be found in
migration and social mobility, which includes both occupational shifts and changes in social status."[5] By concentrating
upon mobility (population change), the urban historian can
relate his findings for a specific city or a specific period in the
history of several cities to a common theme. The study of
mobility involves not only the migration of people into and
about the city, but also their movements within the social and
occupational structures of the city. Since geographical and
social mobility are also the most significant factors in immigration, a common basis for studying the relationship between
urban growth and immigration in the nineteenth century can
be established.[6]

The book that stimulated interest in the quantitative
analysis of urban population mobility and set the example for
the "new urban history" was Stephan Thernstrom's *Poverty
and Progress: Social Mobility in a Nineteenth Century City.*[7]
Thernstrom attacked the myth of social mobility in the nineteenth century, using manuscript census reports and local
property records of Newburyport, Massachusetts. By analyzing the economic, geographic, and occupational mobility of
the urban laborers, he demolished the traditional assumption
that social mobility in the mid-nineteenth-century city was
much greater than it has been in the twentieth century. In later
articles and books he extended his study to include Boston in
the twentieth century and continued to refine his methodology.[8] Although Thernstrom does not concentrate specifically on the interaction between urbanization and immigration,
what he learned about the population of these two cities can
be compared to what is known about the experiences of
ethnic groups in other urban environments.

Peter Knights is another of the new urban historians who
studied Boston, although he preferred the earlier city of pre–
Civil War days.[9] Knights used more sophisticated techniques
of quantitative analysis to prove that high mobility rates were
the rule rather than the exception in antebellum Boston.

Howard Chudacoff broke out of the pattern of studying the large eastern cities with *Mobile Americans: Residential and Social Mobility in Omaha, 1880–1920.*[10] By examining one of the larger commercial centers of the Midwest, Chudacoff helped to fill in one more piece of the puzzle that is the urban process. Other historians are continuing to work on other cities.[11]

The lack of information about urban mobility in cities of different sizes and types in different places and stages of growth has limited the efforts to write broader comparative studies. Adna F. Weber's *The Growth of Cities in the Nineteenth Century* (1899) is still the best general work on urban population movements.[12] More recent is *Cities and Immigrants,* by David Ward, which examines from a broad perspective the national patterns of urban immigration between 1820 and 1920 and compares the residential and employment characteristics of immigrant groups in several large cities.[13] Relying mainly on the work of urban geographers, Ward's book is valuable in delineating the spatial changes that occurred in the nineteenth century under the impact of population growth and industrialization.

Considerable research on the population changes of the urban foreign-born has been done by sociologists. Few of these, however, shed any light on the role of the immigrant in the growth of cities prior to the last few decades. *Social Systems of American Ethnic Groups* by W. Lloyd Warner and Leo Srole is the best known, because of both the mass of information it contains and the criticism it has aroused.[14] Their conclusions have been discredited because they constructed a historical background for the project that was based more on fiction than on fact. By relying upon the personal recollections of older living residents of Newburyport, Massachusetts, in the 1940s, they concluded that ethnic groups in the nineteenth century possessed a high degree of upward social mobility.[15] Thernstrom's study of Newburyport proved that these conclusions were wrong.

One of the earlier historical works that precedes the "new

urban history" but more directly confronts the problem of the interaction between immigration and urbanization is *Boston's Immigrants* by Oscar Handlin.[16] Using literary and quantitative sources, Handlin charted the movement of the ethnic population in three phases: arrival, adjustment, and conflict. Of special interest is the second phase, in which the economic and physical adjustment of immigrants is described. By using federal and local census materials, he was able to locate the immigrants (mainly Irish) in the occupational structure and their subsequent movement, or lack of movement, within the economic life of the city. He concluded that because of their poverty the Irish were heavily concentrated in two unskilled occupations, domestic service and common labor.[17] Apparently stuck on the lowest rungs of the occupational ladder, the Irish failed to rise in the society. In the decades after the Civil War they remained in much the same position as before. A few of the second generation were able to push their way into the skilled and semiskilled trades, but by 1880 the number of Irish in the nonmanual and professional occupations was inconsequential.[18] By uncovering this lack of economic mobility on the part of the Irish, Handlin made it clear what the role of this ethnic group was for the city:

Therein lay the significance of the Irish in the city's economic life. Before their arrival the rigid labor supply had made industrialization impossible. It was the vital function of the Irish to thaw out the rigidity of the system. Their labor achieved the transition from the earlier commercial to the later industrial organization of the city.[19]

Similarly the chapter on physical adjustment is a richly detailed account of how and where the Irish lived and a description of their movement about the city. *Boston's Immigrants* serves a dual purpose of describing the city's influence on the immigrants and the immigrants' effect upon the physical, economic, social, and political development of Boston.

Handlin's book is the best on urban immigration, but there are several other historical studies of eastern cities that touch upon the concept of mobility. Robert Ernst's *Immigrant Life in New York City, 1825–1863* is a multiethnic study which relies heavily upon the state and federal censuses in order to chart the arrival, settlement, and social adjustment of the immigrants in New York.[20] Varying somewhat from the pattern set by Handlin and Ernst, who studied large immigrant communities, Donald Cole examined immigrant life in a smaller industrial city in New England. Cole discovered what he labeled an "immigrant cycle," in which the foreign-born progressed decade by decade from an isolated position to eventual "active participation" in the political, economic, and social life of the broader urban community.[21] Unlike Handlin's study of an earlier period in Boston, Cole's study concluded that between 1865 and 1890 the Irish made considerable progress in the industrial society of Lawrence. The earliest arrivals faced harsh conditions and were forced onto the lowest social and economic levels; but through the establishment of churches, social organizations, and political clubs the ethnic group eventually created for itself a significant role in the life of the city.[22]

Although each of these studies tells us something about the mobility of urban immigrants, their lack of agreement makes it difficult to form meaningful generalizations about the role of the foreign-born in the process of urbanization. Handlin found that the Irish were immobile in Boston, Cole concluded that they were more successful in Lawrence, and Thernstrom proved that the immigrant workers of Newburyport entered the labor scale at the bottom and moved up gradually. Chudacoff found much residential mobility but little ethnic clustering in Omaha, and Humbert Nelli discovered that occupational mobility among Italians in Chicago took place usually within the working class.[23] More studies must be and will be made before we can generalize confidently about the process of urbanization in American cities, and certainly more needs to be known about the role that immigration played. This study examines in depth a city that differs from those previously studied, one in which the forces of immigration, industrialization, and urban growth were clearly interacting: South Bend, Indiana, during the years from 1850 to 1880.

South Bend, being a midwestern city, provides a contrast to the larger urban centers of the Northeast that have already been examined. It also differs from Omaha, which Chudacoff studied, in that South Bend was smaller and became more dependent on industry and immigrants. Without studies of immigration in smaller cities outside the Northeast we cannot know whether the conclusions of Handlin or Cole or others are representative of the general pattern of immigrant mobility or immigrant leadership. Moreover, if Handlin is correct in asserting that the poorest and least talented newcomers were often trapped in the eastern port cities, whereas those with more money and ambition moved on west, we need to know how these talented individuals fared in the cities of the interior. Did they meet with greater economic success or become community leaders more easily than did the Irish of Boston or the Jews of New York? The study of a city like South Bend should provide some clues.

South Bend, unlike other cities that have been studied, was a young city undergoing rapid growth between 1850 and 1880. The total population of South Bend grew from 1,652 in 1850 to 13,280 in 1880, an increase of slightly more than 800 per cent.[24] The number of inhabitants of foreign stock increased from 274 in 1850 to 6,210 by 1880, a growth rate of over 2,000 per cent.[25] Persons more familiar with the proportions of a Chicago or a New York might object that South Bend was still too small to be classified as a city even in 1880. One convenient index to urbanization, however, is that suggested by Kingsley Davis, "the proportion of populations classed as 'urban' in the official statistics of each country."[26] In 1880 the U.S. Census Bureau classified as urban areas all those with more than 10,000 inhabitants. South Bend is a city according to this definition.

Another index of urbanization that made South Bend an attractive city to study is the growth of urban services. Many of the services described by Bayrd Still in his history of Milwaukee are also present in South Bend.[27] In the thirty years before 1880, South Bend experimented with and established a unified water system, street lighting, paved streets, and a police department, and granted a streetcar franchise to a corporation that had been operating since 1873. In addition, private citizens were active in bringing the refinements of urban life to South Bend. The first telephones were installed at the Oliver factory in March, 1878; Studebaker introduced electric lights two years later; and on March 8, 1879, the first two bicycles appeared on the city streets. In general South Bend was establishing much the same type of urban services that were being created by the larger cities of the Great Lakes area.[28]

As a comparatively new city, experiencing rapid population growth and change, South Bend in these three decades before 1880 shows the influence of immigration on urbanization better than do many of the older, more stable, communities of the East. The social and economic patterns or characteristics of the city were still being formed, and the impact of increasing numbers of foreign-born is more visible than in a larger city like New York or an older Yankee city like Newburyport. Furthermore, one can determine the effects of immigration on the physical development of the community and—by examining the residential patterns and the movement of immigrants about the city—determine how these affected the city's appearance. It is important to determine whether ethnically segregated areas appeared early in the community's growth or, if not, at what later stage they began to take shape, and geographic mobility patterns are closely related to other characteristics of a community's growth. As Sam B. Warner, Jr., has suggested, changes in the size of a city and in its social geography seem to have strong influences upon political and municipal institutions, on communications within the city, and on informal associations.[29]

South Bend was undergoing a transition from commerce to industry between 1850 and 1880. Like other cities in the Great Lakes area after the Civil War, South Bend developed industrial potential largely through the exploitation of local water power and, perhaps more importantly, through the technological innovations and inventions of local residents such as the Studebaker brothers and James Oliver. Immigrants (Oliver was from Scotland) played a crucial role in this growth, both in terms of leadership and in providing an abundant labor supply to attract new industries.[30] By 1879 South Bend had grown from a rural village on the banks of the Saint Joseph River to one of the most important industrial centers in Indiana. The Studebaker Corporation, which began in 1852 with a capital of $68, was producing twenty thousand wagons a year by 1879 and had a capital investment of over $3,000,000, the largest in the state. Likewise Oliver's plow factories were producing machinery valued at more than $800,000. The Singer Sewing Machine Company, attracted to South Bend by the abundance of raw materials and labor, was the third major industry of the city, with a production that passed the million dollar mark by the early 1870s. These three manufacturers alone employed more than two thousand workers, most of whom were foreign-born or the children of foreign-born.[31]

By having participated in the three national movements of urbanization, immigration, and industrialization between 1850 and 1880, South Bend has some claim as a representative midwestern city. It obviously differed from its neighbors like Chicago, but the societal processes that affected South Bend and its population were similar to those which influenced other cities of the Great Lakes area, as well as the urban centers of New England and the Pacific Coast. Stephan Thernstrom has stated this problem of "representativeness" most succinctly: "It is obvious that in certain ways every community, like every individual, is *sui generis;* it is equally obvious, however, that cities that are a part of a particular social order are exposed to common influences and display some common characteristics."[32]

By examining South Bend's foreign-born and their descendants we shall see the interaction between urbanization and immigration, and by concentrating upon the central theme of population movement, expressed in terms of physical or geographical mobility, occupational mobility, and social mobility, we shall be able to compare South Bend with other cities.

2

THE GROWTH OF
AN URBAN COMMUNITY

For Henry Barth, merchant, the first issue of the local South
Bend newspaper for the new year 1850 must have brought
some strange feelings of nostalgia and satisfaction. Squeezed
between the advertisements for Wistar's Balsam of Wild
Cherry and Bryant's Indian Purifying Extract were opti-
mistic letters from South Bend migrants to the California gold
fields.[1] Thinking of the several hundred residents who in the
last year had left families and neighbors behind to search for
better opportunities in the West, Barth might have been re-
minded of his own westward journey. Still a young man of
thirty-one, he could have remembered well enough his old
home in Baden, Germany, and the hopes that had stimulated
him to move. The apprehension of the journey to Bremen and
the doubts and hardships experienced in the Atlantic crossing
were probably still fresh memories.

The letters from his former South Bend neighbors may
have brought memories of his own struggle, but Henry Barth
could also congratulate himself on his accomplishments. He
had not only migrated from Germany successfully, but he had
also established himself in a business with a promising future.
Whether from shrewd foresight or previous experience, Barth
had decided to enter the lumber business in this small trading

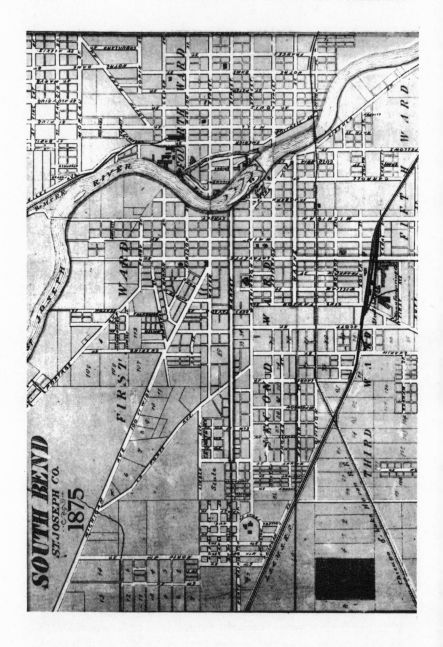

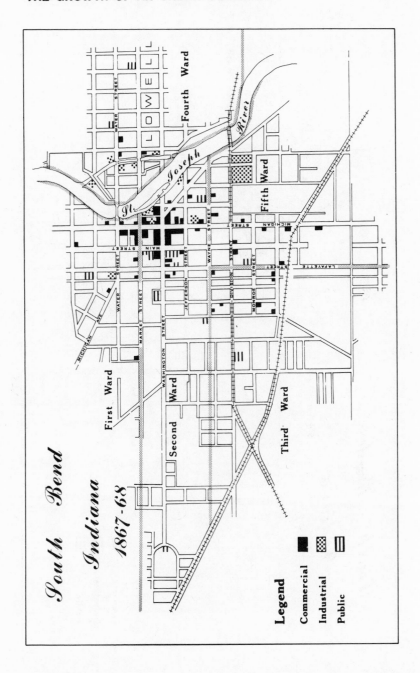

South Bend
Indiana
1867-68

Legend
Commercial
Industrial
Public

First Ward
Second Ward
Third Ward
Fourth Ward
Fifth Ward

St. Joseph River

LOWELL

WATER STREET
MAIN STREET
WAYNE STREET
MICHIGAN STREET
MICHIGAN AVE.
MARKET STREET
WASHINGTON STREET
JEFFERSON STREET
DIVISION STREET
MONROE STREET
LAFAYETTE STREET

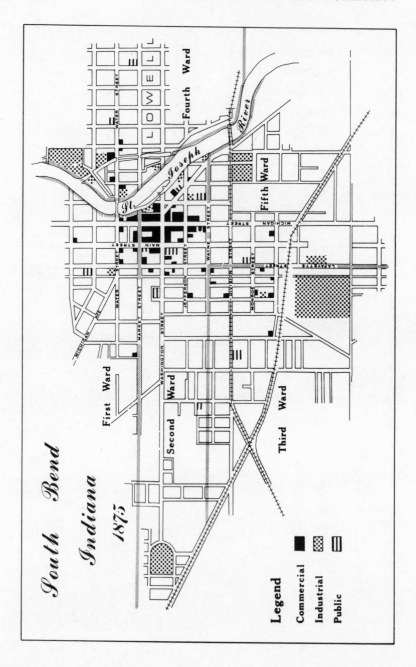

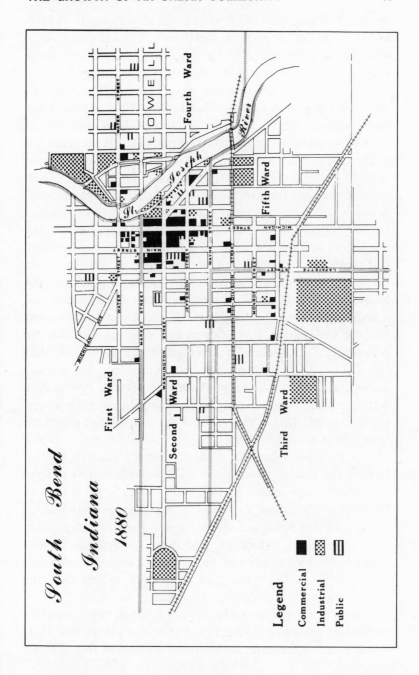

South Bend
Indiana
1880

Legend

Commercial
Industrial
Public

town in Indiana. His establishment was already worth twenty-five hundred dollars by 1850, and during the next thirty years, as South Bend grew and prospered, Henry Barth's real estate and personal property would exceed fifty thousand dollars.[2]

How much men like Barth were aware of South Bend's potential for growth is impossible to know, but for the westward migrant, whether native- or foreign-born, the city at mid-century was not an unattractive place. It was certainly not so exciting or busy as its neighbor, Chicago, nor could it ever hope to become the river city that Saint Louis was (though some of the town boosters would have disagreed). Nevertheless it was a natural commercial center for the northern Indiana region. Alexis Coquillard, agent for John Jacob Astor, had recognized in the spring of 1824 that the site was an agreeable and promising location for a fur trading post. Setting up on the south bank of the Saint Joseph River near a portage to the Kankakee River, Coquillard soon found himself the leader of a small rural community. By 1831, the same year the town was laid out and platted, the residents began to use the river for commerce. Keel boat traffic developed first, but in 1833, after one failure by Coquillard, the first steamboat, the *Matilda Barney,* arrived at the foot of Washington Street. Before 1834 was over, the *Matilda* was facing competition with a new steamboat, the *Davy Crockett,* and the commercial growth of South Bend was under way.[3]

A growing awareness of South Bend's chances for becoming the elusive "Gotham of the West" also seems to have taken hold of the settlers by 1833. The booster spirit of the two hundred residents was expressed in a guidebook that boasted of their twenty brick and frame houses, their two physicians, two lawyers, one newspaper, and three "mercantile stores." Small as the community was, the inhabitants were nevertheless proud of the progress that had been made in less than one decade and were assured that their future was bright.[4]

Boosterism and the active desire to recruit newcomers was undoubtedly aroused by the appearance of a competitor. Only a few miles to the east, A. M. Hurd discovered iron deposits and, in 1834, incorporated the village of Saint Joseph Iron Works on the south bank of the river. After merging the settlement with Indiana City and renaming it Mishawaka, the town promoters built a dam for water power, hoping to attract industry. Despite its efforts, however, Mishawaka was never able to take control of the competition for commerce and industry from South Bend. It displayed signs of modest growth through the 1860s, but after the supply of iron ore ran out and a disastrous fire leveled the business district in 1872, Mishawaka fell far behind. While South Bend was increasing in population by 85 per cent between 1870 and 1880, Mishawaka grew by less than 1 per cent.[5]

In the rapidly developing northern counties of Indiana, South Bend became an increasingly important population center after 1850. While immigration and the birth rate had expanded Indiana's population by 108 per cent between 1850 and 1880, the number of inhabitants in South Bend had multiplied more than eight times. The wilderness trading post established by Coquillard had become the twelfth-largest city in the state by 1860 and was seventh in 1880.[6] Even though Indiana cities were still small if measured by eastern standards, midwestern population centers like South Bend were beginning to experience some of the same patterns and problems of urbanization as their older predecessors to the east.

To meet the problems that increased yearly as more new residents arrived, the town trustees reorganized the political structure in response to a citizens' petition, and South Bend was incorporated as a city in May, 1865. Before the end of the month an election ratified a new municipal charter, and a new mayor, William George, took office in June. To aid the mayor in creating municipal laws and making decisions, councilmen were elected from each of the three wards. Later, in December, 1866, a fourth ward was added by annexing the community of Lowell, which lay directly east of South Bend on the opposite bank of the Saint Joseph River and south of the University of Notre Dame.[7] A fifth ward in the south central part of the city, between the river and Lafayette Street, was created out of the old Third Ward before 1880.

Even with five wards the area of the city for which the new municipal government was responsible was not large in 1865. At its core was a central business district that spread outward from the intersection of Michigan and Washington streets (map 1). This crossroads was a natural center of activity, for here two main arteries for the region met to bring together local residents, farmers from nearby, and travelers from three directions. To the east the flow of traffic was less direct because of the river. Those coming from the east side of the city or from Mishawaka crossed the Water Street bridge two blocks to the north. Michigan Street between Water and Washington, then, became the most heavily traveled route and consequently became the main street of the city.[8]

At this point where transportation routes converged, business activity was most intense and land values highest. From 1850 to 1880 and after, the number of three- and four-story brick buildings steadily increased, pushing the central business district outward along Michigan and west to Main and Lafayette streets. By 1880 this core was composed of dozens of retail stores and small shops (map 4). Bankers and barbers, dentists and druggists, plumbers and publishers all competed for the most favorable locations and stimulated those with capital to build new and larger business blocks. As the business directory grew larger each year, the frontier appearance of the community changed. Stores selling books and musical instruments replaced shops that had sold buckskin goods and buffalo skins only a few years before.[9]

Moreover, as the city grew, small satellite business districts developed around other points of activity or population concentration. Small service businesses such as grocery stores, taverns, and barbershops clustered along Water Street in the Fourth Ward near the Singer factories and paper mills, and in the southern part of the city near the Studebaker wagon factory and the railroad depot another group of small shops served workers and travelers.

As is suggested by the location of these small concentrations of shops and stores, the city developed two distinct areas for industrial use. As long as water was the principal source of power, manufacturers crowded their shops and warehouses along the banks of the two millraces near the center of the city (map 2). Flour mills, small furniture factories, and several foundries were established along the east bank of the river in the 1840s and 1850s. Later some of the most valuable land in this area was acquired by larger manufacturers. In July 1868 the Singer Sewing Machine Company purchased several square blocks of land on the east bank. That same year James Oliver, who was having increasing success with his patents for an improved chilled plow, purchased more land and enlarged his factory on the west bank (map 3).[10]

This pattern of concentration for industry was changed after 1870, when several manufacturers followed Studebaker's example of switching to steam power and located their plants along the tracks of the Lake Shore and Michigan Southern Railroad in the southwestern part of the city. When Oliver, who had formed the South Bend Iron Works in 1855, built a new plant near Studebaker in 1876, the principal manufacturing center of the city shifted to the Third Ward (map 4).[11] These changes altered the appearance of the city not only because a second major industrial area was created, but also because the workers followed their employers to the Third Ward and established homes there. Prior to the 1870s, when the city had one core of economic activity in the business and industrial districts near the river, housing tended to cling as closely to this center as possible. Moreover, residential divisions based on social and economic class or on ethnic origins remained rather weak as long as the city was small. Lowell, or what became the Fourth Ward east of the river, tended to attract artisans and laborers who worked in some of the small mills along the river. On the west bank the First and Second wards, which contained the principal business houses, were populated largely by small shop owners and those who made their living from commerce. But before the 1870s, when the city was still small and its economic life relatively simple, the class structure was dimly reflected in residential patterns. Only after the major industries shifted away from the center of the city and became million-dollar operations employing hundreds of workers did the city develop residential areas clearly based on economic and occupational interests. The Second Ward, especially along Washington and Jefferson streets west of the business district, became the favorite location of the wealthier professional and commercial class. The First Ward between Market Street and the river to the north also became scattered with houses belonging to business and community leaders. At the same time the Third, Fourth, and Fifth wards, which contained the industries, increasingly became the residential sections for the factory workers.

The development of South Bend from a small, homogeneous town that drew its life from rural commerce into a larger, more diversified, industrial city necessitated a growth in urban services, which were at the same time a symptom and an additional cause of urbanization. When Mayor George took office in 1865 most of the basic services that characterize an urban environment were still in elementary stages or were nonexistent.

The first concern of the new mayor and council was the creation of a police department to improve the means of protecting life and property. The professional force that was set up was similar to that developed earlier by Philadelphia or that of New York prior to its Municipal Police Act of 1844. Watchmen in each ward patrolled from twilight to daylight for $1.25 a night. As in New York, this small professional force was supplemented by a watch of local residents, usually merchants. The daytime force consisted of only one marshal in 1865. More night watchmen and special police were added as the city grew and the number and variety of crimes increased. The emphasis on night watchmen was well placed, since a survey of the court activities and crime reports shows that over half the crimes committed involved burglary or theft of some type. The other major crime, assuming that neither slander, "malicious trespassing," illegal voting, divorce, nor bastardy were major crimes, was assault with intent to kill or rape. A typical case was that of Tom Benway, arrested for burglary. After jumping bail and leaving town, Benway was returned and put to work on the city streets wearing a ball and chain. Less typical perhaps was the case of "Bad Kate" Buhler. Kate, a local prostitute, was arrested in Kashmarek's saloon on Chapin Street for fighting with Bill Arndt. The newspaper reported that she was charged with assault but failed to say with what intent. Crimes of assault and burglary continued to increase as the population enlarged, necessitating in 1878 a reorganization of the police department. Professional patrolmen were added to the larger night force, which provided continuous protection.[12]

As police protection steadily increased and adjusted to the enlarged demands, so did other urban services between 1850 and 1880. Newspaper editors were never reluctant to point out the city's needs or to offer direct criticism of the mayor and council if decisions were unnecessarily delayed. A subject of common complaint after the mid-1860s was the condition of the streets. During the nineteenth century, few streets were paved in the residential sections, but in the central business district along Main, Michigan, and Market streets the increased traffic resulted in demands for some sort of paving. Cobblestones were used to pave intersections and gutters in the late 1860s, but proved to be unsatisfactory, because the rough stones caused too much wear and tear on wagons and on drivers' nerves. In the 1870s the city experimented with various other types of paving. Gravel was tried on Michigan Street, but most travelers preferred cedar blocks, which were smoother but less durable. Streets slowly improved as the city matured.[13]

The system of lighting was also adjusted to accommodate an expanding urban community. Until 1868 most of the streets were dimly lit by coal oil lamps. The formation of the South Bend Gas Light Company in August of that year, however, convinced many of the city boosters that theirs was surely one of the most modern cities of its size in the country.[14]

As it was similar to other cities in the development of police and street systems, South Bend was also within the typical pattern of urbanization in its development of fire protection. Prominent citizens and business men looked upon membership in the volunteer fire companies as a sign of acceptance into society. Young businessmen in particular were eager to join units like the Young Hoosier Company and to parade on public occasions in their uniforms: "black broadcloth double-breasted jacket, with gilt buttons, black pants, white belt with red letters and trimmings, and white leather skull cap with black visor and red ornaments."[15] Aside from what the appearance of such a unit of eighteen men must have done to small children and nervous dogs, these volunteer fire companies of South Bend were generally effective, for there were no disastrous fires between 1850 and 1880. Several industries, such as Coquillard's and Studebaker's wagon factories or Oliver's foundry, suffered losses from fire more than once, but never did the city receive a setback like that which Mishawaka experienced when its central business district burned.[16] The most intriguing of South Bend fires was the complete destruction of Saint Joseph's Catholic Church on the day after Christmas, 1872. The cause of the mysterious fire was finally disclosed when an old Know-Nothing fanatic confessed to the crime on his deathbed.[17] Despite a few dramatic cases like this, South Bend had success with a volunteer system. Its continued use was not necessarily an indication of smallness or immaturity, however, for Philadelphia inaugurated a professional fire-fighting department only in 1871, and Saint Paul relied on volunteers until 1881.

When the city was incorporated, a board of health was created to prevent the spread of disease and eventually to establish hospitals. But a hospital could not be built until 1882, and apparently there was not much success in preventing disease. Reports of lung fever (pneumonia) and typhoid made regular appearances in the obituaries of the local papers.[18]

Smallpox was another serious problem that was little affected by the preventive efforts of the board.[19] The progress made toward better health in the community can be inferred from both the *South Bend Daily Tribune* editor's comment in June 1880 that the street gutters were filthy and the board of health's order that citizens remove the filth and garbage from their property. The Third Ward, near the railroads and factories, was described as particularly unhealthy.[20]

Only sporadically did the board receive any aid in its efforts to improve public health. In 1855 local physicians formed the Saint Joseph Medical Society, but it lasted only four years. When it was reorganized in 1875 by Dr. John Sack, there were twenty-three physicians listed in the city directory. Whether all of these deserved the title of physician is a question that perhaps can only be answered by their patients. At least the quantity of medical aid available had increased, if not always the quality. The Denslow brothers, for example, who charged one dollar a visit (two dollars by mail if a stamp and lock of hair were included) to "treat diseases by magnetic power, or the laying on of hands," would not conform to twentieth-century notions of medical practice; nevertheless they were respected in the city and continued to practice and compete with more than a score of other "doctors" for several years.[21]

Like other urban services, communications made modest but significant improvement in the three decades after 1850. In 1848, at the beginning of this period of urban growth, the city had just paid for the completion of a telegraph connection. By 1880 South Bend was attempting to realize its boast of being one of the most modern cities of the West by establishing a telephone system. James Oliver installed the first telephone in 1878, and within the next two years the Telephone Exchange Company "netted the city" with wires.[22]

Similarly, the basic framework of the transportation system, local and regional, developed between 1850 and 1880. Bonfires and cannon bursts celebrated the arrival of the first train from Lake Erie on Saturday evening, October 4, 1851.[23]

This single rail connection with other commercial centers along the Lake Shore and Michigan Southern route was adequate until the 1860s, when industry and trade had increased sufficiently to encourage some citizens to seek a second railroad through South Bend. In 1866 the Peninsular Railroad Company was formed with stock subscriptions totaling ninety thousand dollars. No immediate progress toward a second railroad was made, however, until 1870, when the Michigan Central Railroad Company constructed a line connecting South Bend with the main road at Niles, Michigan. A year later the Chicago and Lake Huron Railroad Company tracks entered the city, thus giving South Bend adequate rail connections to support its growing industries.[24]

As in most American communities in the last half of the nineteenth century, the people moved about the city by horse or by foot. Several livery stables provided hack service, and some by 1880 had installed telephones for the customers' convenience. Calling for a hack was certainly a luxury and was also evidence that life in South Bend was becoming more urbanized, but this was never a form of transportation that was used regularly in the daily movement between home and work. Nor were bicycles a satisfactory solution to the problems of local transportation, even though they were common enough in the 1870s that the city passed an ordinance to keep them off the sidewalks.[25] Rather, it seemed to the community leaders that the only acceptable alternative was to develop some form of an urban railway system. The earliest efforts, beginning with the incorporation of the South Bend Street Railway in June 1873, however, met with only limited financial success. Not until well after 1880, when an electric streetcar system was constructed, could the city claim any improvement in its transportation facilities.[26]

The social development of the city paralleled its physical and economic expansion. Along with the brick business houses, street lights, and factory smokestacks, an urban community with a wide range of social institutions and activities began to appear. For a nineteenth-century town that was not far removed from the rural frontier, it was not surprising that one of the earliest social institutions to develop was the church. The Methodists were the first to hold a public service (in 1831, in the home of Benjamin Ross), but as the population increased, the number and variety of churches multiplied. By 1879 South Bend had at least thirteen separate denominations and some thirty-nine congregations or religious organizations. Saving sinners and encouraging the pious may have been the primary function of the churches, but the many bazaars and socials brought members of the whole community together in a less serious setting.[27]

Much the same spirit that helped to found the churches encouraged the community to establish institutions and organizations to care for its poor. The Benevolent Aid Association, South Bend Union Relief Association, Catholic Aid Society, and Ladies Relief Society all gave assistance to the orphans, widows, and unfortunate poor of the city.[28] Similarly the Saint Joseph County Total Abstinence Society vigorously attacked the evils of drink and tried to stem the proliferation of saloons as the city expanded. After dying out in the Civil War years, the temperance movement surged back strongly in the 1870s as the population of South Bend increased and social control became more difficult. With Schuyler Colfax as chairman and many prominent citizens participating, the temperance society had enough support by 1874 to pack the twelve hundred seats at Good's Opera House.[29]

But if urban growth created increased concern for South Bend's sinners, it also stimulated responsible interest in her scholars. In the first thirty years after Elisha Egbert opened a school in 1831 the town residents relied mainly on a few small parochial schools that the Catholics set up and on the county seminary on West Washington Street. In 1861 a local editor complained that only about half of the city's students were receiving any education in township schools.[30] The urban growth that followed the Civil War, however, stimulated new interest in a better educational system. Madison School was constructed in the First Ward in 1864, and by 1873 the new board of education had provided schools for each of the five wards. The rapid advance in South Bend's educational facilities was recognized in 1873, when its new high school was designated as one of the fifteen in the state that met the new requirements for admitting students at Indiana University.[31]

Private education also kept pace with the expansion of the urban community. Saint Joseph's Academy and Saint Patrick's Grammar School were among the several new Catholic schools that served the growing immigrant communities. Even higher education was not neglected: in addition to the University of Notre Dame and Saint Mary's to the north of the city, there was Northern Indiana College on Washington Street. Likewise a number of special schools like the Spencerian Commercial College and the Classical Institute for French and German languages appeared and disappeared in the 1870s.[32] Interest in libraries also increased, and by 1869 there were at least four private and public libraries serving the community.[33]

The greater social maturity evident in the formation of churches and schools also found expression in a variety of clubs, lodges, and other voluntary associations. Half a dozen Masonic chapters, several Odd Fellows lodges, a historical society, an Audubon Club, literary and musical societies, and an assortment of women's clubs occupied the leisure hours of the residents and fortified their sense of community. Here if anywhere was the key to the developing social system of the young city. In a society characterized by rapid growth and population turnover, these voluntary associations provided some continuity and stability as well as the first hint of a class structure. Young businessmen and newly arrived immigrants alike soon recognized that membership in social organizations enhanced one's chances for upward social mobility.

Moreover, the lodges and societies provided the principal sources of entertainment for the whole community. Concerts, lectures, plays, dances, walking matches, roller-skating parties, and a variety of other entertainments sponsored by local clubs kept boredom at a minimum. The Pleiades Club, a literary society, for example, organized a lecture series featuring Bret Harte, Thomas Nast, Edward Eggleston, and Elizabeth Cady Stanton. For the less serious-minded there were Buffalo Bill's troupe, P. T. Barnum's lecture, "How to Make Money," or the Chicago Comedy Combination at Good's Opera House. The Odd Fellows offered a "georama" of the Holy Land and generously threw in a side show of Robinson Crusoe and his animals.[34]

The most popular type of entertainment, however, was the theater. Here too the social clubs provided the initiative. The local talent of the German Dramatic Society and A. O. Miller's theatrical group could usually pack the Odd Fellows lodge at twenty cents a ticket. With the opening of Good's Opera House in 1867, South Bend began to attract the better talent of the traveling troupes. Professional companies presented popular plays like *She Stoops to Conquer, Factory Girl, Streets of New York,* and *Under the Gas Light,* as well as versions of *Faust* and *Hamlet* played by Edwin Booth. Even burlesque, such as Carrie Duval's "Lady Minstrel and Parisian Sensation Troupe" and Eddie Foy's "Varieties," found its way to South Bend, despite the objections of local moralists.[35]

Such was the city to which the immigrants came. Still in the initial stages of urbanization, South Bend offered the foreign-born opportunities that could not be had in the isolated life along the farming frontier or in the overcrowded cities of the eastern seaboard. Here the immigrant might hope to find a community whose social and economic structure was not already fixed by long tradition. Here the newcomer could avoid the anonymity of the ethnic ghetto and participate in the formation of a new urban community. Perhaps unaware of his role in the social and economic movements of the time, the immigrant could at least sense the optimism and enthusiasm of this adolescent midwestern city.

3

GEOGRAPHICAL MOBILITY

The growth of South Bend from river town to industrial city is a story of men in motion. The population of 13,280 in 1880 was less than half the total of all who had lived in South Bend since 1850. The census enumerators counted nearly 26,000 persons in this thirty-year period, and how many more had come and gone unrecorded in the decennial lists is unknown. The brick business houses and wood-framed homes that gave the appearance of stability and permanence were a mask for the rapid changes and population turnover in the urban community. Old-timers who had been present for more than a decade provided the guidance and direction in shaping the urban environment, but the majority of the inhabitants were newcomers.

Moreover, many who stopped for a time to share in the opportunities that South Bend offered were foreign-born. For one out of every five persons listed in the census schedules, the move had begun somewhere in Europe or Canada. If the second-generation children of the foreign-born are added, the total number of known persons in immigrant families who passed through or settled in the city during these years was 10,143. Thus the process of urbanization in its early stages was carried out not only by a population that was highly mobile, but by one that contained a large proportion of immigrants.

The role that the foreign-born and their children played in the urbanization of South Bend is related to two types of movement. The first is horizontal, or geographical, mobility. This involves the physical movement of persons from Europe and Canada to South Bend as well as their movement within the city itself. By analyzing geographical mobility we can determine who came to the city and by what route they arrived, as well as what impact they had upon physical growth and residential patterns. The other type of movement is vertical mobility, the immigrants' experiences in the social and economic structure of the urban community (see chapters 5 and 6).

The immigrant movement from Europe to the United States is a familiar story and has already been examined by many historians. It was ironic that many who came to live in South Bend and take jobs in the factories there were probably pushed out of their European homelands by the impact of urbanization and industrialization. Some who arrived around the middle of the century may have been refugees of an economic revolution. From England and later from Germany came skilled artisans whose businesses had been destroyed or whose opportunities had been narrowed by the creation of large-scale industries. The reduction in steamship fares to twenty dollars or less by 1861 provided an easy escape for Europeans limited by the changing economy. Cheap transportation also affected European farmers by creating an international market for farm products and a decline in prices. Greater competition, the use of new agricultural techniques, and the higher production costs which came with mechanization all resulted in the transformation of European farming from the quasi-feudal activity of peasants into the commercial operations common to the twentieth century.

What is less well known than the causes of emigration, however, is why and how some of the foreign-born eventually came to South Bend and similar cities of the Midwest. A few who came were motivated not by any previous knowledge of specific opportunities available in South Bend, but by the promotional efforts of the state of Indiana. In 1864 Governor Oliver P. Morton ordered the publication of a pamphlet to promote immigration and two years later intensified his efforts by creating a commission on immigration. These efforts bore little fruit, however, partly because the legislature refused to finance the promotion adequately. Governor Morton's support for immigration failed to increase the proportion of foreign-born residents in the state, which had reached a peak in 1860. Indiana's lack of success in attracting foreigners is illustrated by the fact that only 8,242 immigrants who arrived at Castle Garden between August 1, 1855, and December 31, 1860, named that state as their destination. Illinois, aided by the Illinois Central Railroad in the recruitment of new residents, was the choice of 44,965 immigrants during the same period.[1]

Supplementing the state's feeble efforts, the immigrants themselves informally recruited settlers. The initial settlement of German farmers in Marshall and Saint Joseph counties in the early 1840s, for example, attracted relatives and friends still in Europe. As South Bend and the surrounding communities of northern Indiana developed, letters like that of J. W. Schreyer to his brother-in-law in Germany describing the economic opportunities available in 1846 became more frequent.[2]

More deliberate and systematic recruiting campaigns were carried out by some manufacturers to alleviate the labor shortages of the early 1870s. James Oliver, a principal employer of foreign workers, on one occasion met twelve Polish families in New York in 1875, gave them transportation to South Bend in a boxcar, and built houses for them near the railroad tracks west of Chapin Street. The Studebaker brothers carried on a similar campaign of recruitment and housing for their factory workers.[3]

Whatever the motives for leaving Europe and whatever the reasons for choosing South Bend, the number of first and second generation immigrants in the city steadily increased between 1850 and 1880. As the economic opportunities increased and the social structure of South Bend took shape, the proportion of persons in immigrant families grew from 16.6 per cent in 1850 to 46.8 per cent thirty years later (table 3–1).

Table 3–1
POPULATION OF SOUTH BEND: 1850–80

Census Year	Native-born (Nonimmigrant Families)		Foreign-born		Native-born (Immigrant Families)		Total in Immigrant Families		Total Population
	No.	%	No.	%	No.	%	No.	%	
1850	1,378	83%	124	8%	150	9%	274	17%	1,652
1860	2,616	68	644	17	572	15	1,216	32	3,832
1870	4,763	66	1,229	17	1,214	17	2,443	34	7,206
1880	7,070	53	3,263	25	2,947	22	6,210	47	13,280
Total	15,827	61%	5,260	20%	4,883	19%	10,143	39%	25,970

Source: Manuscript federal census, 1850, 1860, 1870, 1880.

Representative of the foreign-born who were to populate South Bend before 1880 were the forty German families from Augsburg, Bavaria, who arrived by riverboat in 1847.[4] For the next thirty years migrants from Germany were the predominant ethnic group in the city. Driven from their farms by the crop failures of 1846–47 and 1852–55 and attracted by the reports from fellow countrymen already in South Bend, Germans from Bavaria, Baden, Hanover, Hesse, Mecklenburg, Saxony, and Württemberg steadily increased in number with each census.

In most years immigrants from Bavaria, particularly the vicinity of Wunsiedel, were the most numerous, although the number from elsewhere in Germany continued to grow at a moderate rate.[5] Exceptions to this pattern of gradual growth were the immigrants from Prussia, who, in the decade after 1870, rose from 160 to 1,577. Some of the increase can be explained by the expansion of Prussia after 1866 or the unification of 1871. This political change may have caused some immigrants to list their birthplace as Prussia rather than Hesse or Mecklenburg. This is a possible explanation, but it does not appear to be the most realistic one for the immigrants of

South Bend. Properly speaking, these new immigrants from Prussia should not be considered German at all, for it is obvious from the names recorded in the census schedules that they were Polish. The establishment of a Polish Catholic church and several Polish organizations in South Bend after 1870 is additional proof. Of course there was undoubtedly a good deal of mixing between Germans and Poles during this part of the nineteenth century, and without further information it is impossible to determine how many Prussians were more Polish than German. Nevertheless, it does not seem unreasonable to conclude from the census schedules that the Poles were responsible for almost all of the increase in immigration from Prussia after 1870.

Most Polish immigrants were farmers and common laborers driven out of Prussia by the political and economic changes. Carl Wittke has estimated that "only about one in 16 had a trade" when they arrived in the United States.[6] At a disadvantage, the Poles often took whatever employment was available for the unskilled. For some, at least, this meant working for the railroads, and it seems that it was in this manner that the first Poles reached South Bend in the late 1860s.[7] As in such cities as Buffalo, Milwaukee, and Chicago, however, a small community, once established, attracted others of the same ethnic group. Moreover, Polish migration was further stimulated by the active recruitment of Poles by the Studebakers and James Oliver to meet the labor shortage of 1870. Polish workers and their families were imported directly to South Bend.[8] Thus the decade of the 1870s marked the beginning of an increasing flow of Polish immigrants who came to the factories of South Bend; by the end of the decade the foreign-born population had increased by over 1,600, and most of these were Poles.

As German and Polish immigrants increased, they displaced the English-speaking foreign-born as the largest in number, if not in influence. Because their reasons for emigrating were not always similar, the English-speaking foreign-born should be subdivided into three distinct categories. Immigrants from Great Britain (England, Scotland, and Wales) were the second-largest ethnic group in the town in 1850, making up 20 per cent of the foreign-born population (table 3–2). However, although this English portion of the foreign-born community grew consistently, nearly doubling each decade, it failed to keep pace with other groups and by 1880 accounted for only 4 per cent of the foreign-born population. Instead of remaining the second-largest group, the English fell to fourth.

Table 3–2

FOREIGN-BORN IMMIGRATION TO INDIANA AND SOUTH BEND, 1850–80 (In Percentages)

Place of Birth	Indiana				South Bend			
	1850	1860	1870	1880	1850	1860	1870	1880
Germany	54%	57%	56%	56%	40%	50%	55%	70%
Ireland	24	21	20	18	11	24	18	9
Great Britain[a]	13	10	10	10	20	5	6	4
British America	4	3	3	4	20	12	12	8
France	4	5	5	3	7	5	3	1
Switzerland	1	3	3	3	—	2	2	1
Belgium	—	—	—	—	—	1	—	3
Other	—	1	3	6	2	1	4	4
Total	100%	100%	100%	100%	100%	100%	100%	100%

Source: For the statistics on Indiana see Barnhart and Carmony, *Indiana*, 2:299. Percentages for South Bend were computed from the manuscript federal census, 1850, 1860, 1870, 1880.

a. Includes Scotland and Wales.

An English-speaking ethnic group that was able to maintain its position at least in number was the Irish. Like the Poles, the Irish had been pushed out of their native land by an agricultural revolution and economic depression, and many arrived in the United States penniless and with few jobs open to them other than day labor. When large numbers came in the 1850s it was natural for them to turn to the railroads for employment. Hence, like the Poles—who would follow them in larger numbers two decades later—the first Irish immigrants worked their way west with the railroad. The number of immigrants who had been born in Ireland rose from 13 in 1850 to 154 by 1860. This was the decade when the railroads reached South Bend and several nearby villages. From 1860 until 1880 the Irish were surpassed in number only by the groups from Germany, a pattern which resembled that of the rest of the state (table 3–2).[9]

The third English-speaking group was made up of immigrants from British America. In all of the censuses from 1850 to 1880 this was the third-largest ethnic group. To classify the foreign-born from British America as a part of the general English migration is to create some distortion, however, since a number of the Canadians were descendants of the French rather than the English. But as in the case of the Poles from Germany there is no way to separate the two accurately, given the limited information in the census reports. Even in 1880, when the birthplace of the parents of each person is recorded, a majority are second- or third-generation Canadians, and therefore it remains difficult to determine accurately whether they should be classified as French or not. But since Canada and the other provinces were officially a part of the British empire, the immigrants from those areas are referred to here as a part of the English-speaking ethnic community, rather than the French.

The French, of course, were represented among South Bend's foreign-born population, and their role can not be ignored: Alexis Coquillard, one of the founders, was French born. Their community, however, remained small, numbering only thirty-nine at its peak in 1870 and accounting for a bare 1 per cent of the foreign-born population in 1880 (table 3–2).[10]

Of the other ethic groups who made up South Bend's foreign population, most were too small before 1880 to have any strong influence on the city's growth. The number of migrants from Switzerland was never large and failed to increase as the rest of the community expanded. Oliver considered Swedish workers good enough to justify his hiring an agent for Swedish immigration.[11] The Italians and Hungarians, who were later to become of some importance in South Bend, did not arrive in significant numbers until after 1880. More important were the Belgians. A few, like the Buysse and Van Vennet families, had settled in the 1860s, but the census reports show that the majority came after 1870.[12] The Belgian migration actually consisted of two separate movements, one directly from Europe to South Bend, stimulated by the active recruiting of employers like Oliver, the other from nearby Mishawaka, where Belgian immigrants had been employed in the small shops and factories since 1860. When the Milburn Wagon Company closed, several of the Belgian families changed their residence to South Bend, where the opportunities for employment were more favorable.[13]

The experience of the Belgians raises the question of what the internal migration patterns of immigrants were in the United States. If the Buysse and Van Vennet families stopped in Mishawaka before their arrival in South Bend, how many other immigrants must have stopped in other towns or cities before coming to this particular community? Did the majority come directly from Europe, or was South Bend only the second or third stage in a pattern of constant movement?

The few available literary sources suggest that even in the earliest stages of immigration to South Bend there was some movement directly from Europe. After an eleven-week voyage on a merchant vessel, the forty German families brought by John M. Meyer from Augsburg, Bavaria, traveled by canal through New York State and across the Great Lakes to Chicago by steamboat. After one more week on the Saint Joseph River, they stepped ashore at South Bend in 1847. The following year another group of seventy-five Germans made the journey by way of Quebec.[14] The recruiting efforts of Oliver and the Studebakers after the Civil War also suggest that direct immigration from Europe continued throughout the period before 1880.

A more complete picture of migration patterns, however, can be drawn from the manuscript census records. Since the persons studied were only members of families or households

in which one or both parents were foreign-born, an analysis of
the native-born persons in these households reveals the basic
outline of immigrant movement. The census report of the
Rennoe family, for example, contains enough information to
construct a rough map of the family's movements. Joseph
Rennoe was a forty-four-year-old gardener living with his wife
and ten children in the First Ward when the census was taken
in 1880. A Canadian by birth and ancestry, he had married a
woman born in Indiana whose parents were from England
and Canada. The movement of the family is revealed from the
information on their children, however. The first four children,
ranging in age from ten to sixteen, were born in Canada. The
next child, aged eight, was born in Illinois about 1872. This
first migration to the United States evidently was not successful, for three years later, when the next child was born, the

Table 3–3

**BIRTHPLACE OF NATIVE-BORN IN IMMIGRANT HOUSEHOLDS,
SOUTH BEND: 1850–80**

Birthplace (By Region)	Native-born Members of Immigrant Households									
	1850		1860		1870		1880		Total	
	No.	%	No.	%	No.	%	No.	%	No.	%
New England	11	13	21	10	35	8	37	5	104	7
Middle Atlantic	31	37	88	42	175	43	324	47	618	44
South	5	6	9	4	12	3	25	4	51	4
Old Northwest (excluding Indiana)	37	44	91	43	174	43	279	40	581	42
New West	—	—	1	—	11	3	25	4	37	3
Total	84	100	210	100	407	100	690	100	1,391	100
Indiana	66	44	360	63	807	67	2,150	76	3,383	71

Source: Manuscript federal census, 1850, 1860, 1870, 1880.

family was back in Canada. The following year, 1876, they
were in the United States again, this time in Indiana. Whether
this last move was directly to South Bend or first to some other
Indiana community is not clear. Nevertheless, one can see that
through the census information it is possible to trace the paths
of migration at least from state to state.

When an analysis was made of 4,774 persons who were part of immigrant households between 1850 and 1880 but were born within the United States, several patterns of migration were revealed. First, as table 3–3 shows, the greatest number in any census year were born in Indiana. This evidence reflects the natural growth of the resident population, but it also corroborates the literary sources, which suggested movement from Europe directly to South Bend. Especially by 1880, when 76 per cent of all native-born members of immigrant households were born in Indiana, there is strong reason to conclude that immigrants came directly to South Bend without stopping elsewhere. Most of the increase in the foreign-born between 1870 and 1880 resulted when Polish workers sought jobs in the expanding factories. Most children in these Polish families were born either in Prussia or Indiana, which suggests direct migration. Frank Hosinski, for example, a semiskilled plow factory worker in 1880, had four children, age one through nine, all of whom were born in Indiana. An even clearer example is Jacob Andriski, whose two-year old daughter was born in Prussia in 1878, but whose youngest child was born in Indiana in 1879. Obviously the Andriski family had moved directly to South Bend, where the father found employment in a farm implement factory.[15]

Although this hypothesis of direct migration from Europe to South Bend is probably true for the large numbers of Polish immigrants who came in the 1870s, when economic opportunities were expanding, it does not exclude the possibility that some immigrants first stopped in other Indiana cities and communities. The magnitude of the movement from neighboring counties and towns to South Bend cannot be accurately measured by using the census reports, but no doubt such a movement did occur. A pattern of intrastate migration would conform to the law of migration formulated by Adna Weber: "The distance traveled by migrants varies in the same ratio as the magnitude of the city which is their destination. The larger the town, the wider its circle of influence in attracting immigrants. . . ."[16] As long as South Bend was still small its attractive force probably did not extend much beyond Saint Joseph and the immediately surrounding counties. But after the Civil War, when it became one of the leading industrial centers of the state, its power to attract workers would have been increased.

Another ambiguity created by using the census schedules to reconstruct migration patterns occurs for immigrants who were childless at the initial settlement point outside of Indiana. A couple who settled first in New York or Pennsylvania but had no children until they moved to Indiana would appear in the census records to have moved from Europe to Indiana in a single step. Although such occurrences were probably not frequent, they show that generalizations made from census information, although more precise than conclusions based solely upon a few diaries or contemporary observations, may be inaccurate.

If Indiana is excluded from the analysis (in order to eliminate the distortion created by those born within the city), the migration pattern is quite distinct (table 3–3). The immigrant families who settled in South Bend passed through one or both of two regions: the Middle Atlantic and the Old Northwest, exclusive of Indiana. Within these regions the states most frequently mentioned in the census reports were New York, Pennsylvania, Ohio, and Michigan. Also by 1880 the number of children born in Illinois had increased.[17] From this evidence it is easy to confirm the commonly held belief that there were two principal routes for immigrants moving west. One route was through Pennsylvania, possibly along the Pennsylvania Railroad or National Road to Ohio and eventually to Indiana. The wife of Henry Carney, a laborer from Hesse, for example, and his oldest son were born in Pennsylvania, but the younger children were all born in Indiana. Even those whose migration covered a number of years often followed the same basic route. Henry Cahill, an Irish grocer, had children ranging in age from nine to thirty, all born in Ohio, but by 1880 he had moved his family to South Bend.

The other path of migration, mainly for those who had

initially settled in New York, was to the north along the Erie Canal and the Great Lakes. David McNish, a Scottish clergyman with a New York wife and children born in New York and Michigan, had apparently followed this route to South Bend. Both of these avenues of immigrant traffic through New York and Pennsylvania were aided by major railroads which passed through or near South Bend before converging at Chicago.

The movement of immigrants to South Bend was not always in a westward direction. By the 1870s the vanguard of settlement had pushed sufficiently beyond Indiana for South Bend to have benefited from those retreating from the rural frontier. The number of children in immigrant households who were born in Illinois and states farther west increased in the decade before 1880. The pattern of backtrailers like the William Blum family, who retreated from Iowa to Illinois and then to Indiana, was becoming more common. Some, like part of the Van Vennet family, even returned to Europe.[18] Not all of the movement from Illinois to South Bend, of course, represented a return from some western frontier; in part it was a result of the growth of Chicago. Certainly many of the immigrants who moved west from New York or directly from Europe passed through Chicago, and a few may have settled there temporarily.

Immigration to South Bend from regions outside the Middle Atlantic and Old Northwest was not of significant proportion between 1850 and 1880 (table 3–3). Members of immigrant families born in other states made up only 14 per cent of the total. Vermont was the most frequently mentioned New England state, and Kentucky and Virginia were the most important among the Southern states. Barely 3 per cent of the second generation were born in states west of the Mississippi. Although the number from any western state was small, those born in Missouri were predominant, a weak reflection perhaps of the importance of Saint Louis as an immigrant center.

The movement of foreign-born families to South Bend

was by no means always the last step in the migration—in fact, it was common for the large majority to move on. Studies of rural communities in the Midwest have shown that Frederick Jackson Turner was correct in his assertion that high geographical mobility was a characteristic of the frontier. Merle Curti discovered that the persistence rate of farmers and artisans in Trempealeau County, Wisconsin, between 1860 and 1870 was only 25 per cent. In the following decade 29 per cent of the county residents stayed long enough to be counted in two decennial reports. In Wapello County, Iowa, 30 per cent of the inhabitants who were present in 1850 were still there ten years later.[19] But if Turner was not incorrect, he was too narrow in his identification of high geographical mobility with the rural frontier; for other studies have shown that mobility was equally characteristic of cities. Between 1849 and 1859 only 20 per cent of the population in Rochester, New York, remained stable. In Philadelphia, Omaha, Atlanta, Poughkeepsie, and Northampton, Massachusetts, the persistence rates for several decades in the mid-nineteenth century ranged between 30 and 53 per cent. Even for a larger city like Boston only a minority remained long enough to be recorded in two census enumerations. The persistence rates for heads of households in Boston were 44 per cent in the following decade and 39 per cent between 1850 and 1860.[20]

Given this pattern of low persistence in other nineteenth-century cities and along the farming frontier, it is no surprise to find that the foreign-born and their children in South Bend were highly mobile. Fewer than one in five persons in immigrant families who lived in South Bend in 1850 were still there after ten years (table 3–4). Between 1860 and 1870 the out-migration increased, leaving only 16 per cent who were counted in both censuses. As more factory jobs opened up in the 1870s the persistence rate increased to 26 per cent. Over longer periods of time the turnover of the ethnic population was greater, with only 4 per cent who stayed for the full thirty-year period from 1850 to 1880.

Not all of the persons who disappeared from the census

lists moved out of the city: death accounted for some of the turnover in population, and others were lost because of changes in name or variations in the spelling of immigrants' names by the census takers. Nevertheless the rate of change was of such magnitude that the normal death rate and minor errors in the census records would not have effectively changed the migra-

Table 3–4
PERSISTENCE OF ETHNIC GROUPS, SOUTH BEND: 1850–80[a]
(In Percentages)

Place of Birth	Persistence Rates					
	1850–60	1860–70	1870–80	1850–70	1860–80	1850–80
Native-born of immigrant parents	27%	49%	53%	13%	43%	—
British America	—	13	24	—	10	—
English	27	26	30	13	21	13%
Irish	33	5	17	—	3	—
German	19	17	18	3	13	3
Polish	—	—	11	—	—	—
Other European	—	6	15	—	3	—
Total	18	16	26	6	15	4

Source: Manuscript federal census, 1850, 1860, 1870, 1880.

a. Includes only gainfully employed males.

tion patterns. In fact the persistence rates given in table 3–4 represent only the net population change after ten or more years. The gross turnover of population on an annual basis would show even greater movement. Many migrants, for example, moved into South Bend, stayed only a few years or perhaps months, and were gone before the census enumerators could record their presence.[21]

Why the immigrants moved on or where they went are difficult questions to answer. Some no doubt were attracted to other communities where the chances for success seemed better than in South Bend. More than one hundred foreign- and native-born residents left for the Colorado gold rush in 1859, and a similar number followed the next year. Likewise the growth of Chicago in the latter half of the nineteenth century must have drawn workers away from South Bend.[22] But once they leave South Bend they are lost from view, and no attempt has been made to follow their continuing movements.

The occupational and economic characteristics of those who chose to stay in South Bend for at least ten years will be examined in detail in chapters five and six, but table 3–4 shows that some ethnic groups were more inclined to stay than others, even though no group can be described as stable. The native-born children of immigrants were the most persistent, and this reflects the tendency of immigrant families, especially those with several children, to be less mobile than single individuals. The higher persistence of the native-born was also a result of the fact that they adjusted more easily to the American environment and usually found better jobs than did their parents. In fact the whole pattern of ethnic persistence seems to be closely related to the occupational and economic, as well as social, experiences of the foreign-born in South Bend. The English and Germans, who were most likely to stay, were often the skilled craftsmen and businessmen who accumulated modest resources in capital and real estate. The Poles and other Europeans, who appear to have been less stable, were concentrated primarily in semiskilled and unskilled occupations.

South Bend was a restless community: for the Germans and English, who came in the 1850s and 1860s, and the Poles, who came after 1870, South Bend was less a home than a way station. The proportion of any ethnic group willing to stay for as long as a decade was seldom more than one out of five. Coming by way of the Great Lakes or moving westward through Pennsylvania and Ohio, they stopped for a time to test South Bend's opportunities, then moved on to try again elsewhere. The majority of the participants in this sketch are really only dim silhouettes drawn in the pages of the census records by the hands of local census takers. Some stayed' to leave a more lasting mark on the community, but most did not.

4

RESIDENTIAL MOBILITY

Regardless of the route they followed or the time they stayed, all immigrants faced similar problems once they arrived in South Bend. Less awesome than New York or bewildering than Chicago, South Bend nevertheless posed formidable problems for the newcomer. One of the first concerns was where to live. Unfamiliar with the neighborhoods and sometimes low in capital, the immigrant probably experienced a brief period of moving about until he decided where he could or should live.

For those with no friends or relatives who could provide temporary shelter there were various hotels and boarding houses. The Saint Joseph Hotel, a four-story brick building at the corner of Main and Washington streets near the center of town, offered room and board for as little as $2.50 per week in 1856.[1] By 1880 the South Bend House, Union House, Kunstman House, Oliver House, and a variety of smaller establishments provided temporary homes for immigrants. Some, like the Kunstman House, which was owned by an immigrant, or the European Hotel on South Main, were filled almost entirely with foreign-born workers employed in the local wagon factories and foundries.[2] It was not uncommon to find hotels or boarding houses that were dominated by a single nationality. Two-thirds of the twenty-two boarders at the South Bend

House in 1880 were German, and the only three native-born
residents had parents from Bavaria or Prussia (table 4–1). In
1870, twenty-nine of thirty-three boarders in the house of
Frank Burr, an Austrian, were foreign-born. All, except four
Danes, were from Germany.

Table 4–1
NATIONALITY OF BOARDERS AT THE SOUTH BEND HOUSE: 1880

Name	Place of Birth	Occupation
M. Lenz	Luxembourg	Physician
Michael Bechner	Hesse	Blacksmith
John Charlton	Canada	Sewing machine factory
Jacob Merkert	Bavaria	Cabinet maker
Gustav Rooker	Bavaria	Baker
William Wagner	Bavaria	Blacksmith
William Shasock	Prussia	Wagon maker
Charles Early	England	Sewing machine factory
Henry Borden	Canada	Cabinet maker
Edward Ziverson	Austria	Cabinet maker
Conrad Nuff	Hesse	Works in dress manufacture
Adam Blacksmith	Wisconsin (parents, Bavaria)	Blacksmith
George Wolf	Bavaria	Wagon maker
John Kepkie	Germany	Painter
Henry Hoffon	Pennsylvania (parents, Prussia)	Bookkeeper
Jacob Baker	Hesse	Carpenter
George Berter	Württemberg	Machinist
John Haker	Indiana (parents, Prussia)	Sewing machine factory
Joseph Schick	Switzerland	Plow factory
Maggie Lefern	Bavaria	No occupation
Ester Celavan	Prussia	Domestic
Joseph Lucoski	Prussia	No occupation

Source: Manuscript federal census, 1880.

But the manuscript census shows that it was more common for two or three boarders to live with an immigrant
family than for immigrants to live in the large boarding houses
or hotels. In 1880, the first year that the enumerators recorded

the relationship of inhabitants to the head of the household, 4 per cent of the immigrant population were classified as boarders. Although this rather low percentage might suggest that not many immigrant families took in boarders, the actual situation has been somewhat obscured by the census taker's methods. Usually if two or more families were living in the same house the enumerator did not distinguish between owner and boarders, instead recording each family as a separate household and designating each person's relationship to the head of that particular family. Only by comparing the number of "heads of the household" in the census records with the number of dwellings can we arrive at a description of the housing patterns. In 1880, even though the number of boarders listed is small, there is an average of one and one-half "households" or families per dwelling: thus the multiple-family dwelling was common for a large number of South Bend immigrants in 1880, and detailed examination of the census reports suggests that the same was true for preceding years. Often the families that lived in the same house were relatives and part of an extended family. Young couples with children often lived with parents, who also might still have children at home.[3]

Despite the doubling up of immigrants there is little indication that housing was exceptionally poor or overcrowded in this mid-nineteenth-century city. Some of the newcomers were forced to rent one-room shanties or to live in tenements upon their arrival, but by the 1870s conditions were improved. Oliver and the Studebakers helped to alleviate overcrowding by building houses that they rented to their workers. Oliver in fact had a policy of encouraging home ownership. It is doubtful that these company houses were either as spacious or as elegant as the Gothic Revival home which Horatio Chapin built in 1855; nevertheless, before 1880 one finds no complaints about slum housing in the city.[4]

Even with more than one family living in the same house, there does not seem to have been much overcrowding. In 1850 the average number of persons living in an immigrant

house was only 4.33, less than half the Boston average of
9.16.[5] By 1880 the density had increased to 7.18 persons per
immigrant dwelling—still below the average for Boston and
most other large cities.[6] The First Ward, which contained a
number of hotels, was the most densely populated, with an
average of 9.74 persons per house in 1870, but this had declined slightly to 9.56 by 1880. At least in this period between
1850 and 1880 the increase in immigration did not lead to
serious overcrowding.[7]

Perhaps as important as knowing how the immigrants
lived is knowing where they lived and why they settled in
particular parts of the city. To understand the relationship
between urbanization and immigration it is essential to know
how intensely immigrants were clustered in certain sections
of the city. The geographical distribution of ethnic groups
within the city and their subsequent movement or lack of
movement would be a strong factor in the assimilation of immigrants and in the formation of the shape and character of
the city. It is a common belief among historians and social
scientists that the ethnic ghetto was a stable neighborhood in
which the immigrant found security and protection. As each
ethnic group prospered and matured, its members moved toward the outer rings of the city, where they began to mingle
more freely with the native-born. The older and usually de-
teriorating core was left to new arrivals who were just beginning to be assimilated. This is the pattern of movement
described by Robert E. Park and supported by several urban
historians.[8]

This pattern may have been true for some cities like
Chicago, which Park studied, but it was not true of all. Philadelphia, for example, in the mid-nineteenth century, seems to
have contained few if any ethnic ghettos; nor did it follow the
classic pattern that placed the more affluent on the periphery
of the urban area. Instead—as Sam Bass Warner, Jr., found—
in 1860, when there were many foreign-born in Philadelphia,
the "immigrants were rather evenly distributed between core

and ring." Not until the latter part of the nineteenth century, when intercity transportation improved, did Philadelphia begin to develop residential districts that were segregated on the basis of foreign birth, race, and economic class. More recent studies of Chicago and Omaha have also shown ethnic cluster- ing to be less characteristic of nineteenth-century cities than was previously believed.[9] The evidence from these larger cities suggests that ethnicity did not always determine where new arrivals settled. Occupation and proximity to place of work were initially the strongest influences in determining residential patterns. Only later, when the distance between home and work ceased to be important, did such other factors as ethnicity and class become the criteria for deciding where to live.

Since Chicago, Philadelphia, and Omaha differed in pat- terns of immigrant settlement, it is necessary to ask how other cities, smaller and at different stages of growth, were affected by the increasing numbers of Europeans. Did the foreign- born of South Bend face restrictions in their choices of homes? Were they guided by ethnic consciousness, or were occupations and cost of housing the motivating factors in their selections? The information from the census schedules helps to focus this aspect of the city's past.

There are several valid methods of measuring the magni- tude of residential clustering or segregation. For simplicity in computation and ease in understanding, the method used in determining the unevenness of South Bend's population was the index of dissimilarity and a variation of it, which is called simply an index of segregation.[10] The index of dissimilarity compares the ethnic groups to each other and to the native- born on the basis of their place of residence, which is listed in the census schedules by wards. The spatial relationship of the different groups is expressed in a single, easily readable num- ber, with a range of 0 to 100. Perfect residential distribution or the absence of segregation is represented by 0; complete segre- gation is indicated by 100. Thus if the index of dissimilarity between two population groups is 35, then 35 per cent of one of the groups would have to move to a different area of the

city in order for the two groups to be equally distributed.
The index of segregation is a variation of this method in that
it compares one group to *all others* instead of comparing two
single groups.

Table 4–2

**INDEXES OF SEGREGATION FOR NATIVE AND FOREIGN-BORN
POPULATIONS, SOUTH BEND: 1870–80
(By Ward)**

Place of Birth	1870	1880
Native-born (nonimmigrant family)	14.7	22.3
Native-born (immigrant family)	14.5	14.7
Great Britain	7.1	15.7
Ireland	16.5	32.1
British America	42.9	28.1
Germany (excluding Prussia)	14.0	18.4
Prussia	10.2	44.9
Other European	5.1	12.8

Source: Manuscript federal census, 1870, 1880.

As can be seen in table 4–2, the segregation of any single
ethnic group was not great either in 1870 or in 1880, after the
total number of foreign-born and their children had increased
to almost 47 per cent of the population.[11] In each year the least
segregated groups were those classified under the title Other
European. This suggests that the Swedes, Belgians, Swiss and
others in this category faced the fewest restrictions upon their
choice of residence or were least influenced by ethnic ties and
thus in a position to be more easily assimilated into American
society. It would be misleading, however, to try to read this
conclusion into the results. Rather, it must be admitted that in
this case the index of segregation does not provide an accurate
measurement. The category Other European differs from the
others in that it is a general classification and includes several
ethnic groups which may or may not be similar. No single
group in this category was large enough to merit a separate
index. Instead, the degree of segregation can be seen by examining the census reports for the total number of each group

present in each ward (see Appendix, table A-1). These results show that none of the Europeans in this classification were very well distributed throughout the city, either in 1870 or 1880. In 1880 the Belgians lived almost exclusively in the Second and Third wards. Of the thirty-seven Belgians living in the Second Ward, no fewer than twenty-seven lived on a single block on West Washington Street. Six houses contained single families, but the seventh, that of Hest Colfax, was the home of six boarders, all young single men from Belgium employed at the "iron works" (Oliver). In the Third Ward the Belgians were less tightly clustered along Chapin, Ford, and Tutt streets. All but two of the men in these families were employed by Oliver. Quite probably they were living in the houses that Oliver had built for his workers. If so, the choice of residence was determined more by occupation and place of employment than by a desire to live in a neighborhood that was ethnically homogeneous.[12]

The French were concentrated in the Fifth Ward, the Danes and Dutch in the First, the Hungarians in the Fifth, and the Swiss in the First and Fifth. Only the Swedes were evenly distributed throughout the wards. Small but nearly equal numbers of immigrants from Sweden lived in the First, Second, Third, and Fifth wards. Nevertheless, if one examines the Swedes more closely, according to street rather than ward, it is clear that even they lived in rather small clusters. For example, seventeen Swedes lived on the same block on Dunham Street near Oliver's plow factories—again because James Oliver built houses for his immigrant workers. Even though the number of immigrants classified as Other European was small, the location of their homes suggests a pattern of settlement. Some clustering according to ethnic origins occurred, but occupations and place of employment were apparently strong factors also. If ethnic subcommunities existed within the city, they should be most apparent in the larger groups, such as the Irish, Germans, or Poles.

The ethnic segregation indexes for the other categories in table 4–2 are more accurate than for the Other Europeans

because they are based upon generally homogeneous populations. One such homogeneous group, Great Britain (England,
Scotland, and Wales), conforms to the residential pattern that
would be expected according to the traditional interpretation.
Although the index more than doubled between 1870 and
1880, the degree of segregation was still not large enough to
indicate that the British had established a distinct ethnic
community. No examples of English or Scotch families
clustered together on the same street were found in the census
schedules.[13] In this pattern South Bend was similar to other
cities, like New York.[14] The British role in the social structure
and leadership of the community will be taken up later, but at
this point it seems clear that group consciousness was of minor
importance in the selection of a place to live.

The same, however, cannot be said about the other two
English-speaking groups, the Irish and the immigrants from
British North America. In fact the opposite is true. The Irish
and British Americans (largely Canadian) were two groups for
whom a cohesive bond resulting from consciousness of kind
was most evident. From 1850 to 1880 these immigrants lived
in small but recognizably ethnic neighborhoods. In 1854, when
Father Alexis Granger of Saint Joseph's Parish took a census
of his church members, he counted 46 families containing 299
people. Of the 46 families, 30 were French and 16 were Irish.
The majority were living in Lowell which later became the
Fourth Ward of South Bend on the east side of the river.[15]
Although Father Granger spoke of French parishioners, he
probably meant French Canadians. (There were never many
immigrants who reported their place of birth as France; the
greatest number occurred in 1870, when there were 39, of
whom only 3 lived in the Fourth Ward.[16] In the same federal
census, however, the enumerator counted at least 87 Canadians
with residences in that ward.)

Later parish censuses, such as the one in 1868, which lists
the names and addresses of each family, show that the
Canadians and Irish were not only still concentrated in the
Fourth Ward but were separated into two distinct neighbor-

hoods. Walking westward from the river along Water Street one would first pass the houses of the Canadians, like the Archambeaus, interspersed with the homes of native Americans and other scattered nationalities (see map 1). Edwin Turnock, carpenter and life insurance agent from England, lived at 30 East Water, not far from A. T. Coquillard, real estate broker and descendant of the city's founding father. On reaching Hill Street the observant census taker might notice a subtle change in the nationalities of the residents. There was still a mixture of Bavarians, native Americans, and a few Canadians, but after Hill Street, families with Irish names began to appear with greater frequency. Passing Saint Louis, Saint Peter, and Notre Dame streets as well as Saint Joseph's Church one could clearly see that this was a neighborhood dominated by the Irish. It was not exclusively Irish, for there were still Germans and a few Canadians; nevertheless, the area well deserved its local nickname of Dublin.[17]

The federal census schedules confirm the results of the parish censuses and place the residential patterns of the Irish and Canadians in perspective with regard to the rest of the city. In 1870, 62 per cent of all persons born in British America were living in the Fourth Ward (see table 4–3). Even in 1880 this ward still contained 45 per cent of those from Canada, Nova Scotia, and New Brunswick. The Irish, however, appear to have settled not only in the Fourth Ward but in the Third as well. In fact the Irish had been divided into two nearly equal settlements since they first began to arrive in significant numbers in the 1850s. Besides those in Saint Joseph's Parish to the northeast across the river, another settlement around Saint Patrick's Church was located in the Third Ward near the railroad tracks in the southwest part of the city. Although the evidence is not clear, the division of the Irish communities was probably related to employment. Those in the northeast, who were predominately common laborers and menial service workers, were possibly employed by the University of Notre Dame, which was within easy walking distance at the northeast edge of the city. Sorinsville, an area several blocks north of Saint

Joseph's Church, consisted of twenty-five families, most of them employed by the university.[18] The Irish in the Third Ward appear to have been factory workers or employees of the railroad, which they had helped to build.

Table 4–3

PERCENTAGE OF FOREIGN-BORN, SOUTH BEND: 1870 and 1880 (By Ward)

Place of Birth	1870 Ward			1880 Ward				
	1	2, 3ª	4	1	2	3	4	5
Native-born (nonimmigrant family)	18%	66%	16%	18%	30%	15%	16%	21%
Native-born (immigrant family)	22	49	29	18	17	29	22	14
Great Britain	18	55	27	19	26	9	21	25
Ireland	3	63	34	3	13	39	34	11
British America	5	33	62	15	21	9	45	10
Germany	32	50	18	28	23	11	23	15
Prussia	12	70	18	6	16	65	3	10
Other European	23	56	21	16	31	27	5	21
Total	19%	61%	20%	16%	24%	24%	17%	18%

Source: Manuscript federal census, 1870, 1880.

a. The census taker failed to distinguish the Third from the Second ward in 1870.

If ethnicity—either as a desire to live in an ethnic neighborhood or as involuntary restriction preventing immigrants from living in other neighborhoods—was a significant factor in the choice of residence in South Bend, it would seem to have been active among the Irish and the French Canadians. Whether voluntarily or not, these immigrants were clustered more tightly than most other groups. Of the two the Irish were more inclined to cling together in ethnic neighborhoods. The Canadians were still somewhat segregated in the Fourth Ward as late as 1870, but, as the index of segregation (table 4–2) shows, the degree of their segregation declined by more than ten points before 1880. As South Bend became industrialized and factories were built in parts of the city away from the river, the British Americans began to move out of their old neighborhoods in the Fourth Ward. Moreover, the new immigrants from British America who came in the 1870s did not settle in the Fourth Ward but chose to live in other parts of the city. The single decade from 1870 to 1880 was one of great growth and change for the city, and the response of the British Americans seems to have been a movement away from the old neighborhoods, where there had been some tendency toward concentration.

The Irish, on the other hand, appear to have made no such response. In fact, lack of mobility on the part of the Irish caused them to become more segregated in 1880 than they had been in 1870. Exactly the same proportion of Irish continued to live in the Third and Fourth wards. Even the new immigrants from Ireland did not alter the residential patterns of the Irish community. Thus increased urbanization and industrialization tended to undermine and dissolve the attraction which ethnic neighborhoods had for the Canadians but evidently had no influence on the Irish. This lack of response by the Irish in South Bend is quite unlike that of the Irish in Boston, who began to move out of their old neighborhoods near the center of the city as soon as urban transportation was expended and made less expensive.[19] Perhaps this difference between South Bend and Boston could be explained by the fact that the Irish in Boston suffered from a higher degree of overcrowding and thus had a greater incentive to escape to outlying areas. In the Third and Fourth wards of South Bend the housing density was never more than 6.7 persons per house. Although they appear to have been developing one of the more distinct ethnic communities in South Bend by 1880, the Irish were never as segregated as their brethren in Boston. In terms of residential distribution or physical separation from the rest of the urban society, the Irish of South Bend only seem segregated when compared to the generally even distribution of most other immigrants.

Dublin was the nickname for the Irish neighborhood, and

west of the river on the north edge of the city was Goose Pasture. Named after the flocks of geese owned by the early Germans, who moved there in the 1840s, this section of the First Ward above Water Street retained the reputation and something of the flavor given to it by its first residents. There, at the garden of the Turnverein, where Michigan Street met Marion Street, the Germans gathered for an afternoon of sports to celebrate the Fourth of July in 1873. In the evening a grand ball brought together not only Germans but English and native-born as well.[20] But even if the social life of the Germans continued to be active in the First Ward, where the Turners' hall stood, the Germans showed no lasting desire to live there. Without parish censuses for the First Ward and with city directories only after 1867, how concentrated the Germans were in the early years of the city remains uncertain; but in the years after 1870 German immigrants and their children dispersed throughout the city. Even in 1880, when the segregation index shows a slight increase from 14.0 to 18.4, the First Ward contained only 28 per cent of the German population; the Second and Fourth wards each had 23 per cent of the German immigrants; no ward had less than 11 per cent (see tables 4–2 and 4–3). Furthermore, the tendency of Germans from the same states in the old country to cling together was quite weak. For example 43 per cent of the Bavarians lived in the First Ward in 1870, but by 1880 they were evenly distributed, with only 29 per cent living in the First Ward. All of the increase in the number of Bavarians in the city was in the other four wards. The same lack of concentration in a single ward was characteristic of other Germans, such as those from Hesse and Württemberg. According to the city directories and the 1880 census schedules, which sometimes contained street addresses, the Germans—unlike the Belgians—were apparently not significantly segregated in small neighborhoods within each ward.

The startling exception to the normal pattern of even distribution was the segregation of the Prussians in 1880. In 1870, when the Prussian immigrants seem to be of German background, the degree of spatial separation from other groups, native and foreign, was not great. Somewhat like the Bavarians, who favored the First Ward, on the north side of the city, the Prussians were most numerous in the Second and Third wards near the business district (Appendix, table A-1). Nevertheless, there is no evidence that they had attempted or been able to form a distinct ethnic community.

But the decade of the 1870s was the decade in which immigration to South Bend from Central and Eastern Europe began, and most of those after 1870 who cited Prussia as their place of birth were Polish. The total number of "Prussians" leaped from 160 in 1870 to 1,577 ten years later (table A-1). Most of this increase was absorbed by the Third Ward, which had over a thousand Polish residents (63 per cent of the total). Wards One, Four, and Five each had fewer than a hundred immigrants of Polish descent. As table 4–2 shows, the index of segregation rose from a relatively low index of ten in 1870 to a high of forty-six in 1880.

The concentration of Polish Americans in the southwest portion of the city, principally the Third Ward, was characteristic from the beginning of Polish settlement in the early 1870s. The seventy families that Father Adolph Bakanowski estimated were present in 1871 were clustered near the railroads and factories south of Wayne Street and west of Lafayette. The Polish neighborhood rapidly expanded westward along Division Street, and by 1877 the Poles had built Saint Joseph's Church on West Monroe between Chapin and Scott streets, which was approximately at the center of the Polish settlement.[21]

Other segregation indexes confirm the residential patterns outlined in table 4–2. The data in table 4–4, which compares the immigrant's residence with his father's place of birth, are almost identical with previous conclusions. The similarity between tables 4–2 and 4–4 suggests that the residential patterns of the second generation immigrants varied little from those of their parents. (Indexes based on the father's place of birth are somewhat limited, however, since the necessary information on the specific place of birth of the parents is available only for 1880.)

Another test of spatial separation based on ethnic origins, the index of dissimilarity, which compares individual groups to each other rather than to the whole, also supports the previous analysis (see table 4–5). The Irish and the Poles (Prussian) became increasingly separated from other ethnic groups as well as from the native-born, while the German, English, and Other

Table 4–4

INDEX OF SEGREGATION, SOUTH BEND: 1880
(By Residence and Father's Place of Birth)

Father's Place of Birth	Index
Native-born (nonimmigrant family)	22.5
Native-born (immigrant family)	18.3
Great Britain	17.6
Ireland	34.5
British America	44.8
Germany	21.9
Prussia	46.4
Other European	15.3

Source: Manuscript federal census, 1880.

Europeans underwent less change between 1870 and 1880. The Germans and English remained stable in relation to each other and to the native-born. The general distribution of these two groups and their predominance—especially that of the Germans—in the First and Second wards near the central business district indicate in a crude way the degree of their assimilation into the community. Germans and Englishmen were among the earliest arrivals, establishing themselves as businessmen and skilled craftsmen when the town was just beginning its growth as a commercial center. By the 1870s, when the pace of immigration was accelerated by Central and Eastern Europeans seeking jobs in South Bend industries, the older immigrants were already firmly established in the better commercial and residential districts. Consequently, newer residents tended to settle near the periphery, which was rapidly expanding.[22]

TABLE 4–5
INDEX OF DISSIMILARITY, SOUTH BEND: 1870 and 1880

Place of Birth	1870							1880						
	Native-born Non-immigrant Family	Immigrant Family	Great Britain	Ireland	British America	Germany	Prussia	Native-born Non-immigrant Family	Immigrant Family	Great Britain	Ireland	British America	Germany	Prussia
Native-born (non-immigrant family)														
Native-born (immigrant family)	17							20						
Great Britain	11	6						10	21					
Ireland	18	19	15					42	22	43				
British America	46	33	35	39				30	27	24	31			
Germany	16	11	14	29	44			17	18	13	39	22		
Prussia	6	21	15	16	44	20		50	36	56	32	56	54	
Other European	10	8	6	20	41	9	13	13	21	23	41	40	30	38

Source: Manuscript federal census, 1870, 1880.

   The clearest conclusion that can be formulated from any of the segregation indexes or from the census information is that the physical separation between ethnic groups was increasing by 1880. The increase was moderate for the Germans and English but significantly larger for the Irish and the Poles. Ethnic ties were apparently binding enough to keep some of the Irish from leaving the Fourth Ward after the major industries had moved, and the Polish immigrants were clearly more inclined to cling together than the Germans who came before them. The Canadians were something of an exception in that their degree of residential segregation generally declined (tables 4–2 and 4–5). Although the reasons are unclear, it was perhaps because of the changing nature of immigration from British North America. Many of the earliest arrivals were French Canadians, who clustered in Frenchtown along the river in the Fourth Ward.[23] These were the French Catholics counted by Father Granger in his parish census of 1854. Later, when industry expanded and moved to the Third Ward, many of the Canadian immigrants were of English or Irish background and consequently felt no attraction to the French Canadian community that had been established east of the river. Instead they settled in the Second, Third, and Fifth wards, where the opportunities for employment were more abundant.

   Nevertheless, no description of the tendency of some groups to concentrate in certain parts of the city can hide the more obvious fact that segregation of housing based on ethnic origins was weak in 1850 and only slightly stronger in 1880. None of the segregation indexes was greater than fifty during this period, and for most groups the degree of spatial separation was much smaller. No easy generalizations about immigrants clinging together in ethnic neighborhoods can be made to explain why Edward Buysse, a Belgian, lived at 32 Water Street, a more fashionable area of the First Ward, instead of on Washington Street, where most of the other Belgians lived; or why Charles Radatski and Lawrence Skelly lived in the north part of the city near the German Goose Pasture instead of in the neighborhoods that were predominantly Polish or Irish. There are always exceptions to historical generalizations, especially when they involve masses of population, but in South Bend there were too many exceptions to support a conclusion that ethnic origin was the primary factor in the choice of a place to live.

Because the evidence for residential clustering based on ethnicity is weak, a logical alternative is to examine in more detail the trend suggested by the housing patterns of the Other Europeans. The residential clustering of the Belgians, Swedes, and others seems to indicate that the occupation of the family breadwinner was an important factor in deciding where to live. The division of the Irish into two communities, one near the University of Notre Dame, the other near the railroads, is a further indication that even among the groups where ethnic clustering was present, occupation was a principal consideration. Likewise the concentration of the Poles in the Third Ward may have initially been stimulated by the occupational opportunities available when they first arrived, rather than by a desire to create an ethnic neighborhood.

To examine the effect of occupations on residential patterns we first need to describe the occupational structure of the city. Classifications or ranking schemes of the mid-twentieth century can not of course be applied directly to the occupations practiced in a midwestern city a century ago. Some jobs no longer exist, and some have certainly changed in terms of prestige: the harnessmaker or livery stable owner would clearly have been a more important person in 1870 than a century later.

A highly accurate ranking scheme based on the relative social prestige of each occupation probably can never be achieved, but a classification system determined by type of work is easy to construct. Using a classification system suggested by Stephan Thernstrom (who was completing a study of mobility in Boston) and making appropriate adjustments to fit the types of work found in South Bend, one can organize the variety of occupations listed by the foreign-born and their children into eight broad sategories (for an example see Appendix, table A-2).[24]

The first five categories are made up of nonmanual workers, those usually designated as the white-collar classes. At the top of the occupational scale are the professionals—teachers and editors as well as physicians—and the major proprietors, managers, and principal government officials. These two categories of professionals and businessmen contain many of the most important social, economic, and political leaders. The third category consists of semiprofessionals, such as nurses, photographers, or newspaper reporters. The clerical and sales category contains a wide range of white-collar workers from store clerk and bank cashier to mail carrier and traveling salesman. The last nonmanual class consists of the petty proprietors, managers, and officials and includes factory foremen as well as small shopkeepers.

The manual occupations have been divided into three levels. The skilled craftsmen, who occupy the top rank, were clearly in a superior position to other manual workmen. The skilled worker was the man who possessed a special trade— the mason, shoemaker, blacksmith, carpenter, or tailor. Particularly in a young city that was not too far removed in space or time from the frontier, the skilled workman received more respect than he might have received in older eastern cities.

On the lowest levels of the occupational hierarchy were the semiskilled and unskilled workers. Similar in status, the two were significantly different in the regularity and stability of their employment. The semiskilled worker in South Bend was most often a factory worker who possessed some skill that made his labor more valuable than the common laborer's. Painters and varnishers, for example, could usually find steady employment in the wagon factories or at the Singer factory, where cabinets for sewing machines were made. The common laborer, on the other hand, did tasks requiring no special skill that could be done by nearly anyone with a strong back.[25] Hired by the day or week, the unskilled worker had little security or respect. Not only was his employment irregular, but the pay was hardly enough to maintain a decent standard of living. In Saint Joseph County in 1879 a semiskilled planing mill worker received $1.62 a day, but the common day laborer received only $.91.[26] Unskilled laborers were clearly at the bottom of the occupational ladder.

By applying these occupational categories to the information from the manuscript census and noting the ward location of each worker, one can measure the relation between an immigrant's type of work and his place of residence. It will be possible to determine whether the immigrants and their children were clustered according to the type of work that they performed.

As might be expected in a city that was just undergoing urbanization and where industrialization was also occurring, the most immigrant workers were employed in manual occupations for each of the census years examined. In fact the percentage of those who worked with their hands remained surprisingly uniform for all four years: 83 per cent in 1850, 82 per cent in 1860, 85 per cent in 1870, and 81 per cent in 1880 (see Appendix, table A-2). Likewise, in each of the wards in 1870 and 1880 the overwhelming proportion of workers were in manual occupations. But these facts tell us only that the immigrants occupied the lowest levels of the occupational hierarchy in any part of the city. The perspective is too broad to reveal any recognizable patterns. If, however, we look more closely at the eight basic work categories, certain distinctions become more apparent.

Using an index of dissimilarity to measure the spatial distance between the residences of workers in each occupational class, one finds much the same trend that was found before when ethnic origin was used as the determining factor (table 4–6). Since none of the indexes was above forty-six, the separation between occupational classes was not great; nevertheless, there is again a noticeable increase in the degree of separation during the decade of the 1870s. The professional class lived closest to the proprietors, petty proprietors, and

Table 4–6
INDEX OF DISSIMILARITY OF IMMIGRANTS, SOUTH BEND: 1870 and 1880
(Comparing Occupations and Residences)

	1870								1880							
	Professional	Proprietors, Managers, Officials	Semi-professional[a]	Clerical and Sales	Petty Proprietors, Managers, Officials	Skilled	Semiskilled, Service	Unskilled, Menial Service	Professional	Proprietors, Managers, Officials	Semi-professional[a]	Clerical and Sales	Petty Proprietors, Managers, Officials	Skilled	Semiskilled, Service	Unskilled, Menial Service
Professional		14		24	13	16	26	20		14		33	24	17	46	26
Proprietors, managers, officials				11	3	15	15	26				28	19	16	38	23
Semi-professional[a]																
Clerical and sales					11	17	20	25					16	17	36	9
Petty proprietors, managers, officials						12	12	23						8	24	9
Skilled							3	11							30	13
Semi-skilled, service								11								32
Unskilled, menial service																

Source: Manuscript federal census, 1870, 1880.

skilled workers in 1870. Ten years later the professionals, proprietors, and skilled craftsmen were still living in relative proximity to one another, but there was a greater disparity between the homes of the professionals and those of the shopkeepers and managers of the fifth category. This change suggests not only that as the immigrant population grew, the professionals, major businessmen, managers, officials, and skilled workmen remained geographically stable, but that the smaller shopkeepers and lesser city officials were taking up residence in other parts of the city.[27] As the immigrant population rapidly increased in the Second, Third, and Fifth wards, where new factories and workshops were being built, the number of small grocery stores, saloons, barbershops, and shoemakers also multiplied there to serve the local neighborhoods. In 1868, for example, only two out of the total of seventeen grocery stores were located outside the central business district along Michigan, Main, and Washington streets (see map 2). By 1875, however, ten of thirty grocery stores were located outside the First and Second wards. Six of these were operated by immigrants, and most of the proprietors lived in or near their shops.[28] The same pattern holds true for drugstores, tobacco shops, barbers, and butchers. These shops were somewhat scattered, although there were small shopping districts that developed along Water Street near the factories in the Fourth Ward and near the railroad depot in the Third Ward (see map 4).

The larger business houses of the immigrants and native-born remained in the central business district, and their owners continued to live nearby. John Lederer and John C. Knoblock, one an immigrant, the other the son of an immigrant, were the owners of the largest wholesale and retail grocery business in the city; both lived on Lafayette Street near the center of South Bend.[29]

The skilled workers also continued to live primarily in the older part of the city—28 per cent in the First Ward and 27 per cent in the Second. Even though they were in manual occupations, these craftsmen held a more respected and stable position in the community because of their skills and because they were among the principal property owners. In 1850 and 1860 skilled workers owned the largest total amount of real estate; in 1870 they were second only to the businessmen.

Table 4–6 also shows that there was no appreciable increase in the separation between the homes of clerical and sales workers and the homes of the small businessmen and skilled laborers. The indexes for these groups remain essentially the same for 1870 (eleven and seventeen) and 1880 (sixteen and seventeen). The explanation is quite simple if one keeps in mind that most of those who were store clerks and salesmen were young men in their first occupations. At least two-thirds or more in every census year were between the ages of eighteen and twenty-nine, and many were the sons of small shopkeepers who worked in the family store. Hugh and John Cahill, ages thirty and nineteen, for example, were both employed as clerks in their father's grocery store at the corner of William and South streets.[30] Others were the sons of skilled workmen who, perhaps, were trying to improve their status by moving into a nonmanual occupation.

The effect of the city's increased industrialization on residential patterns, however, is clearest in the case of the semi-skilled immigrants. Only the third-largest group behind the skilled and unskilled workers until after 1870, this category contained 45 per cent of the immigrant working population by 1880 (Appendix, table A-2). These were the workers in Oliver's plow factory, in the wagon shops of the Studebaker brothers, and in the smaller industrial workshops of the city. As the major industries expanded and changed from waterpower to other power sources, they moved to the southwest edge of the city, where land was cheaper and there was more room for growth. Near the river, the Fourth Ward, which had been a center for industry until the late 1860s, experienced an actual decline in the number of workers living there. New immigrants were attracted to the southwest part of the city, where jobs were available and Oliver and the Studebakers had begun to provide housing. By 1880, 41 per cent of all semiskilled workers were living in the Third Ward. If the workers in the Second and Fifth wards, which were also near the factories, are counted, one finds that 85 per cent of the semiskilled immigrants had homes in the southwestern section of South Bend.[31] Clearly industrialization was creating a greater division between the factory operatives and all other immigrant working groups.

In fact there is even a growing separation between the residences of the semiskilled and unskilled. Although the semiskilled were increasingly attracted to the Third Ward, the common day laborer felt no such attraction. The unskilled immigrants continued to be scattered throughout the city, finding work where they could, sometimes as streetworkers, carpenters' helpers, or, in the summer, farm laborers. Since their jobs were often temporary, their place of work changed frequently, and no one area of the city offered many advantages over any other. Furthermore, a significant number of unskilled workers were single men living in boarding houses or with other families, who took up lodgings wherever they could.

The empirical evidence concerning residential patterns and mobility points to several conclusions about urbanization and immigration in South Bend. In the earlier commercial city of the 1850s and 1860s, when urban growth was moderate and immigration had not reached its highest levels, the interaction between immigrants and the city was not expressed in dramatic changes. The newcomers did not alter the appearance of the city by clustering into ethnic ghettos, and the community seemed willing to absorb the foreign-born with little fanfare or conflict. German and English businessmen or craftsmen chose homes near their places of work in all parts of the city. Belgians, Irish, and French Canadians gathered together in small groups in several neighborhoods, but residential divisions based on ethnicity were not highly visible even to the local residents.

A significant change, however, occurred in the decade of the 1870s as industrialization and immigration increased. The new immigrants, especially those from Polish Prussia, were

attracted to South Bend as the need for semiskilled factory
workers increased. But just as the change in location of large-
scale industries like Studebaker and Oliver created new economic and land-use divisions between the central business
district and the new industrial section of the Third Ward, the
arrival of new immigrant laborers caused greater residential
divisions. The concentration of over four-fifths of the semiskilled workers in the southwestern section of the city by 1880
meant that the community was more distinctly divided along
occupational lines. Since South Bend had not yet developed
cheap public transportation, most workers still had to be
within walking distance of their jobs.

The conclusion that residential patterns in South Bend
were increasingly influenced by occupations after 1870 must
be modified by the knowledge that ethnicity began playing a
larger role at the same time. For the Poles and other new
immigrants who sought jobs in South Bend industries the
choice of housing might have been based on the desire to live
near fellow countrymen as much as on the desire to live near
the place of employment. As the evidence in chapter 6 suggests, the later immigrants had a stronger tendency to cluster
in social and religious organizations and at the same time were
more often victims of ethnic prejudice. Which was the more
important factor in residential patterns after 1870—ethnicity
or type of work—is not clear from the historical records. What
is clear, however, is that South Bend was becoming a more
divided community as urbanization, industrialization, and immigration intensified.

5

OCCUPATIONAL MOBILITY

On the fifth of July, 1880, James Oliver, looking from his office window on Chapin Street, could see his workers returning to their jobs after the brief holiday. Most were on foot, making their way along the streets deep with mud from the past week's heavy rains. As he watched, Oliver might have wondered if the second half of the year would bring more labor unrest to the city's industries. The first threat of trouble had surfaced in 1879, but Oliver's firm refusal of the workers' demands had prevented a strike. When fifty of his molders were successful in stopping work at the South Bend Iron Works in the spring of 1880, Oliver fired the strike leader and called in the sheriff and other citizens to break up the strike. To a man who still spent long hours in the factory himself and whose personal hero was Napoleon, the thought of knuckling under to his own employees must have seemed absurd.[1]

Oliver's confidence in the American doctrine of hard work and individualism had been molded by his own personal experiences. The eighth child of a Scottish shepherd, James Oliver was born on August 28, 1823, in Liddisdale, Scotland. Like his younger and more famous countryman, Andrew Carnegie, he was brought to the United States as a boy and started at the bottom. After a year in Seneca County, New

York, his family moved to Indiana, finally settling in Mishawaka in 1836. As a teenager working at odd jobs he must have taken to heart the advice he found in *Poor Richard's Almanac,* for by 1840 at the age of seventeen he entered business with a contract to dig a pipeline trench in Mishawaka. In 1845 he began his apprenticeship in the foundry business and a decade later he moved to South Bend to set up his own establishment. Struggling against the financial losses caused by several fires and against strong competition from several other firms, Oliver first revealed the inventive genius that would eventually make him a success when, in 1857, he patented a new process for hardening plowshares. His real technological breakthrough, however, came in 1867 when, after years of experimenting, he perfected a method for chilling mold boards for plows. From this patent grew Oliver's eventual success and fortune. By 1880 when James Oliver acted quickly to put down the strikers, he was protecting a corporation valued at nearly one million dollars and employing over six hundred workers. It had branch offices in Indianapolis, Dallas, and Mansfield, Ohio, and Oliver's name and his chilled plow were known to thousands of American farmers.[2] As an example of the immigrant's success in pursuing the American Dream, James Oliver was surpassed by no one in South Bend and by few others in the country.

There were other success stories among the children of South Bend's foreign-born. Less than two blocks from the Oliver home was the two-story red brick house of John C. Knoblock with its large yard and attractive iron fence along Market Street, an imposing home for one of South Bend's leading businessmen. Like Oliver, Knoblock had arrived in South Bend as a young boy with no advantages other than his own intelligence and ambition. His father had been a weaver in Strasbourg but had given up his trade to become a farmer in Ohio in 1829. Evidently tired of the farm life in Ohio and Indiana where he had been born and reared, Knoblock walked to South Bend in 1848 and began working as a teamster for ten dollars a month at Harper's flour mill. Moving quickly, he left the flour mill to become a grocery clerk and by 1853 had begun his own grocery business in partnership with Kasper Rockstroh. For the next thirty years Knoblock was one of the dominant figures in the city's growth. A Republican and a Mason, he was on the town council that organized the city government and was also prominent as a county official. By 1871 with an estate worth at least $75,000, he had already branched out from the grocery business to organize a flour mill and a furniture factory. His vice president in the furniture company was Schuyler Colfax. Being a stockholder in the Citizens National Bank did not prevent him from participating in the founding of the Saint Joseph County Savings Bank and serving as its treasurer. In 1875 Knoblock became a competitor with Oliver when he and three others formed what was later called the South Bend Chilled Plow Company. With at least a hundred workers, the company produced over 10,000 pieces of agricultural machinery in 1878.[3] Thus when John Knoblock retired in 1882 at the age of fifty-two he was one of the wealthiest and most important leaders in the South Bend community.

Immigrants and their children found American society to be a fluid system open to those with ambition and a willingness to work hard. Apparently the urban frontier was merely a substitute for the rural frontier, in which thousands of migrants had found abundant economic and social opportunities. But such conclusions—based on impressions—no longer offer a satisfactory answer to the questions about social mobility in American society. Enough studies have been made to suggest that the American dream of success was too often little more than that—a dream. Certainly examples of immigrants who failed to succeed in South Bend could be cited to offset the success stories of men like Oliver and Knoblock. But, as Stephan Thernstrom has acknowledged in his study of Newburyport, "a handful of instances cannot reveal what *proportion* of the laboring population . . . reaped the benefits of social mobility, nor can it indicate what *avenues* of social advance were of particular significance to the working class."[4] Only a quantitative analysis of the careers of hundreds or thousands of immigrants will reveal the patterns of vertical mobility.

The advantages of a statistical study of immigrant mobility are matched by the pitfalls, not the least of which is the difficulty of constructing a valid method of measuring the elusive condition commonly referred to as social mobility. The solution most often turned to by historians and sociologists is the use of occupational mobility as an equivalent to or at least as the most significant measure of social mobility. Occupational information for the period between 1850 and 1880 is readily available in the form of the manuscript census reports and can easily be analyzed systematically. Moreover, in American society, whether in the nineteenth century or the present, occupation has been one of the key factors in definitions and theories of class structure.[5]

Occupational mobility, as it is commonly defined, is a change from one occupational class to another. Using the eight basic work categories mentioned in chapter four, one could consider an immigrant like Knoblock, who moved from grocery clerk to owner of his own business, to be upwardly mobile. Conversely, the owner of a small business (such as a restaurant) who changed to a semiskilled factory job would be downwardly mobile. The opportunities for movement of some groups are necessarily more limited than for others. The professional, for example, can only move downward, but the unskilled worker can only move upward. Changes within these broad categories—for example from brickmason to carpenter or from one employer to another—will be treated as representing no change in status even though there may have been some economic difference to the worker. (It is possible, for example, that some larger employers paid higher wages than smaller ones.) Information on wages paid by individual employers in South Bend, however, is not available. Similarly, there may be some inaccuracy caused by the fact that a skilled worker might have been financially better off than a small businessman. Despite these weaknesses created by the lack of more specific information on each individual, the study of occupational changes can yield valuable results.

Typically the study of occupational mobility is of two types: intragenerational, the tracing of the careers of individuals from one census to the next, and intergenerational, the study of occupation changes between fathers and sons. When occupational mobility is examined in both ways, comparisons can be made between first and second generation immigrants. Admittedly, however, such an analysis, which deals only with those individuals persistent for two or more censuses, neglects the experiences of those who moved on. Perhaps those who did not remain—a majority of the working force for any decade before 1880—found success in other cities. Perhaps they did not. In any case, once they left South Bend they were lost from sight. Likewise the study of occupational mobility is by necessity restricted to the male working force. The mobility of the city's gainfully employed females is impossible to trace accurately because of name changes when women marry. Although a few women owned significant amounts of property, most did not, nor did they have any recognizable effect on the occupational structure by being employed outside the home. Even in 1880, when there were 316 female immigrants or daughters of immigrants with jobs, over 50 per cent were employed as domestics.[6]

For perspective on the experiences of the male wage earners who remained for more than one decade, a description of South Bend's economic development and occupational opportunities is essential. Although the growth of business establishments in South Bend is difficult to measure because of the lack of records and the incompleteness of city directories (which began to appear only in 1868), there were still plenty of opportunities available in the 1870s, when the city's population began to increase rapidly. The city directory of 1867–68 lists approximately 227 separate businesses, a number that had increased by at least a third by 1880. Most of the increase was in the number of shops and stores that provided the basic goods and services required by a developing urban community. Few if any new types of specialty shops appeared in 1880 that were not already present a dozen years earlier. Rather, the increase was in the number of barbershops, cigar stores, drugstores, livery stables, and hardware stores. The number of grocers, for example, increased from 17 in 1868 to 28 in 1880.

Furthermore, if one looks not only at the total increase in the number of businesses but at the turnover of individual establishments as well, business opportunities for new residents were probably even greater. Of the twenty-eight stores that sold groceries in 1880, twenty-five had been opened between 1868 and 1880. Only three of the older establishments, one that of John Knoblock, were still operating by 1880. The same holds true for other businesses like dry goods stores or even saloons and billiard halls: the total increase and the high turn-over suggest that the new migrants to the city could find opportunities to enter business if they had the necessary skills and capital to invest. And, since the majority of the city's businesses were not large, the amount of money needed to open a new establishment was not great. In 1879 the average value of stock in a hardware store in Saint Joseph County was only $650, and there were seldom more than one or two employees (who worked for an annual wage of about $312).[7]

South Bend's mercantile establishments continued to grow in response to the demands of an increasing population, but in the years 1850 to 1880 the most dramatic changes took place in its industries. The earliest industries were primarily based upon the processing of agricultural products that were grown in the surrounding county. Flour mills and breweries collected along the banks of the Saint Joseph River, where waterpower and transportation were readily accessible. Flour milling continued to be of some importance after 1850, but South Bend's potential as a milling center for northern Indiana was obviously limited by the growth of Chicago. In 1860 three mills in South Bend shipped out over five hundred thousand dollars worth of products, but by the late 1870s the production rate had not increased, and there were still only three mills in 1879.[8]

Although the processing of flour and such other agricultural products as wool and wood pulp for paper continued to be significant, the greatest expansion was in the industries that manufactured wagons, farm machinery, sewing-machine cabinets, and furniture. The initial stimulus for industrialization was provided by the demands of the Civil War. The Studebaker brothers, who had held several small government contracts before the war, benefited directly from army contracts in the 1860s. Their reputation for building high quality carriages and durable farm wagons was firmly established in a national market by the time the war ended. Their success opened the eyes of other local capitalists, and soon a number of wagon factories were in operation. Others, like A. C. Staley and Sons, who produced blankets and flannels for the Union army, moved to South Bend to take advantage of the transportation facilities and the expanding pool of labor. A sign of the city's prosperity during the war years was the establishment of the First National Bank of South Bend in September, 1863.[9]

Reflecting the "pronounced westward thrust of industry" in the nation after 1865, South Bend increased the number and size of its industries in the late 1860s.[10] Not all of the growth was unplanned, for in 1867 local businessmen organized the South Bend Hydraulic Company and began to rent water power to a growing number of manufacturers. This act, coupled with developments in several key industries (such as Oliver's patent for the chilled plow in 1867, the establishment of a branch of the Singer Sewing Machine Company in 1868, and the incorporation and enlargement of Studebaker Brothers Manufacturing Company in the same year) marked a breakthrough in South Bend's conversion from commerce to industry.[11] By 1875, even after a national depression, in which several local firms collapsed, the value of industrial production had jumped to over $4 million and the number of employees in manufacturing plants had passed two thousand.

Considering this rapid industrial growth between 1850 and 1880, it is hardly surprising that not only did the patterns of immigration change and the number of newcomers greatly

increase, but the overall occupational structure of the immigrants shifted as well. Certainly, the interaction between the
forces of industrialization and immigration was clearly at
work to alter the size of the city and the economic positions
of its inhabitants. Undoubtedly new immigrants were initially
attracted by the expansion and recruiting efforts of well-known
manufacturers like Studebaker, Oliver, and Singer. But conversely the growing pool of labor acted as a stimulus to the
formation of many new industrial establishments. By 1880
there were at least four producers of agricultural machinery
besides Oliver and three more wagon factories, competing
with Studebaker.[12]

The crucial question, however, is how this multiplication
of jobs that came with industrial and urban growth affected
the occupational patterns and mobility of the city's foreign-
born families. Although many earlier studies agree that rapid
urban expansion has led to significant changes in social mobility patterns, there has not been agreement as to the nature
of the changes.[13] Studies that support the blocked mobility
hypothesis have suggested that industrialization limited the
occupational opportunities open to those in manual jobs. As
mechanization eliminated the need for some skilled workers
these craftsmen and their children had no choice but to accept factory positions and a subsequent decline in status. Recent research, however, of which the most convincing is again
that of Stephan Thernstrom, suggests that the new semiskilled
factory positions were filled not by older members of the
artisan class, but by new arrivals, for whom jobs in industry
actually signified an improvement in status.[14] The failing of
earlier studies was that they generalized about social mobility
without adequately evaluating the concurrent geographical
movement of workers into and out of the city.

The experience of the immigrant wage earners in South
Bend seems to confirm Thernstrom's basic conclusions; but it
is easy to understand how previous historians misunderstood
the mobility patterns of nineteenth-century cities. Putting
aside for a moment the investigation of inter- and intragenera-

tional mobility of identifiable individuals who were present for more than one census, and looking only at the aggregate of employed males, the impression is that the occupational structure was becoming more rigid and the opportunities for immigrants more limited as industrialization intensified. In 1850, for example, when the city's immigrant wage earners numbered fewer than one hundred, only 10 per cent were employed in semiskilled positions, not all of which were in manufacturing (table 5–1). But thirty years later, when the immigrant work force was over two thousand, half of the wage earners in immigrant families were working as factory operatives. Meanwhile the proportion of immigrants and their sons in professional, skilled, and proprietor classes declined in the decade of the seventies, the same period in which the most dramatic expansion of industries took place. Working solely from the changes that took place in the overall immigrant occupational structure it is easy to see how one could conclude that opportunities were becoming more restricted as industrialization increased.

Table 5–1

OCCUPATIONS OF IMMIGRANTS, SOUTH BEND: 1850–80
(In Percentages)

	Percentage in Occupation			
Occupation	1850	1860	1870	1880
Professional	7%	2%	3%	2%
Proprietors, managers, officials	5	5	6	3
Semiprofessional	—	—	1	—
Clerical and sales	4	4	3	4
Petty proprietors, managers, officials	25	9	5	4
Skilled	29	30	35	22
Semiskilled and service	10	23	22	52
Unskilled and menial service	21	28	26	13

Source: Manuscript federal census, 1850, 1860, 1870, 1880.

But if one adds the dimension of geographical mobility, the conclusion seems less certain. The downward adjustment in the immigrant occupational structure was strongly affected by the arrival after 1870 of several thousand Poles, Belgians, and Swedes, most of whom came directly to South Bend from the farms of Europe. The large majority of these newcomers lacked the capital or the training that would have enabled them to become part of the business community or independent craftsmen. Consequently they clustered in industries where no investment was needed and basic skills were quickly acquired. And since they outnumbered the older ethnic groups already present in the city, the effect was to reduce the proportion of workers who were employed outside of semiskilled jobs.

Moreover, the fact that ethnic groups like the Poles concentrated in industrial work did not necessarily mean that they were downwardly mobile. Even though it may not be possible to measure the change in status between two entirely different societies, from European peasant to American factory worker, it is certain that industrialization provided better opportunities and a higher occupational position than these untrained immigrants would have enjoyed in the preindustrial city. Before the number of South Bend's factories multiplied, the unskilled immigrant worked as a common laborer, perhaps assisting a carpenter or brickmason, more often as a seasonal hand on the surrounding farms. For such hard physical labor he would have received a daily wage of between $.61 and $.91. For work as a semiskilled employee in one of the factories, however, he could earn $1.25 or more a day.[15] Therefore in one very large segment of the immigrant population in South Bend, the recent arrivals during the 1870s, industrialization provided the means for upward mobility rather than downward.

This hypothesis is reinforced by table 5–1, which shows a marked decline in the proportion of workers in unskilled labor or menial service. Before 1880 approximately one out of every four immigrants was unskilled. This pattern abruptly changed, however, as the opportunities in the manufacturing plants opened up. There were only thirty-two more unskilled workers in 1880 than there had been in 1870, and their percentage of the immigrant working force dropped to thirteen.

The entire change in the occupational hierarchy of South Bend's ethnic population, however, cannot be explained simply by the arrival of new immigrants. If we remove the distorting influence of the large numbers of semiskilled workers who came in the decade of the 1870s, we can examine the effects of industrialization on the ethnic groups that were present before the transition to industry. The Germans, for example, who were among the first of the foreign-born to settle in the city, were represented in all types of work even though the majority in any decade held manual positions (Appendix, table A-2). In 1870, when the influence of significant industrial growth was becoming noticeable, 39 per cent of the Germans were skilled craftsmen. Although this proportion declined to 31 percent by 1880, the change was not great, and the number of skilled workers was still almost equal to the number who were semiskilled. The ratios of English, Irish, and British Americans in skilled and factory jobs varied somewhat, but the picture is essentially the same. In other words, those ethnic groups that were already established before industrialization began appear to have been far less affected than the newer arrivals. Moreover, some skilled workers who changed to factory jobs may in reality have continued doing the same type of work. Although the census reports obscure it, establishments like Studebaker and Oliver employed skilled carpenters and blacksmiths in addition to large numbers of semiskilled workers.[16]

That fewer members of the older ethnic groups were employed in nonmanual and skilled occupations by 1880 reveals only that the overall structure had changed; but in the strict sense this does not shed much light on the process or direction of occupational mobility. Conclusions based on aggregate numbers of workers in various types of employment in different decades are valuable in illustrating the general evolution of the city's economy and the role immigrants played as groups, but such conclusions fail to account for the fact that the German workers who were there in 1880 may not have been the same German workers who were there in 1850 or even

1870. The fact that the proportion of skilled English workers dropped from 53 to 28 per cent by 1870, whereas the semi-skilled increased from 11 to 30 per cent, does not necessarily mean that English carpenters and blacksmiths accepted a decline in status and went to work in the factories (Appendix, Table A-2). It can merely mean that skilled workers simply moved on to seek better opportunities elsewhere. Therefore, although the general work patterns of the immigrants were changing, the occupational mobility patterns of the city's residents remain unclear. Since we have already shown that persistence rates of South Bend immigrants were quite low, any generalizations that do not recognize this rapid turnover are misleading.

The occupational mobility of those who remained in the city for more than one census decade can be measured in two ways: by tracing the mobility of the first generation of foreign-born workers and by comparing their experiences to those of their sons, the second generation, who were born in the United States.

Since South Bend's immigrants were highly transient, the study of intragenerational mobility involves only a minority of the working population in any decade. Moreover, those who stayed were in most cases better prepared to compete for the best jobs in the labor market. Lawyers and businessmen were usually more stable than shoemakers or factory workers. Even in the seventies, when industrial jobs were more abundant, blue-collar laborers were more transient than white-collar workers. The persistence rates among immigrants for 1870–80 were 38 per cent for professionals, 28 per cent for business-men, managers, and officials, 50 per cent for semiprofessionals, 27 per cent for clerks and salesmen, 24 per cent for petty pro-prietors, managers, and officials, 17 per cent for skilled, 11 per cent for semiskilled, and 13 per cent for unskilled workers. In this respect the experience of South Bend's foreign-born workers was similar to that of the foreign-born in other cities.[17]

South Bend was not similar to all other cities, especially those of the industrial Northeast, in regard to the occupational mobility rates of the foreign-born who continued to live in the city. Since the work categories for South Bend's wage earners were modeled on those used by Professor Thernstrom and since the number of foreign-born workers was about the same, a valid comparison can be made with Newburyport. Table 5–2, which compares the occupational progress of persistent foreign-born workers in manual occupations, reveals surprising results. The immigrants in blue-collar jobs who stayed in South Bend for more than one decade were far more successful in achieving a higher occupational status than their counterparts in Newburyport. Of those who persisted for at least one decade in Newburyport, the proportion who rose to nonmanual positions was usually less than one in twenty. In South Bend, however, entry into the white-collar class was much easier for the foreign-born. Between 1860 and 1870 for example one in every three who began in a manual occupation held a white-collar job ten years later. A similar contrast occurs among those who rose to or maintained positions as skilled craftsmen. But the greatest difference between the two cities was in the proportion of persistent immigrant wage earners who occupied the lowest category of unskilled laborer. In Newburyport the proportion of blue-collar workers who held unskilled jobs was always more than half, and for the 1870 census group it was as high as 84 per cent. In South Bend, however, only a minority—14 to 26 per cent—occupied the lowest rung on the occupational ladder.

Table 5–2

INTRAGENERATIONAL MOBILITY OF FOREIGN-BORN WORKERS IN MANUAL OCCUPATIONS FOR NEWBURYPORT, MASS., AND SOUTH BEND: 1850–80

	Occupational Status Attained									
	Unskilled		Semiskilled		Skilled		Nonmanual		Number in Sample	
Year	South Bend	Newbury-port	South Bend	Newbury-port	South Bend	Newbury-port	South Bend	Newbury-port	South Bend	Newbury-port
	1850 Census Group									
1860	14%	72%	29%	8%	43%	14%	14%	6%	8	36
1870	0	55	0	14	100	14	0	18	1	22
1880	0	70	0	20	0	0	100	10	1	10
	1860 Census Group									
1870	17	83	17	5	37	10	30	2	30	54
1880	29	74	13	15	29	5	29	5	24	38
	1870 Census Group									
1880	26	84	28	4	34	9	13	4	80	82

Source: Manscript federal census, 1850, 1860, 1870, 1880; and Thernstrom, *Poverty and Progress*, p. 100.

This radical contrast raises some serious questions about occupational mobility patterns in nineteenth-century American cities. Professor Thernstrom has argued that his conclusions about the low rate of mobility in Newburyport are representative of mobility patterns in other industrial cities, even in those, like New York and Boston, which were much larger.[18] But if his conclusions are correct, how can the mobility rates of South Bend's immigrants be accounted for? One possibility might be South Bend's size. Thernstrom has admitted that the "greatest variations . . . are likely to be found not in the great cities but in the small towns. Even in 1900 the United States still contained quiet villages and market towns in which the factory and the immigrant were unknown."[19] Although South Bend was small by comparison with other cities, at least before the 1870s, it was not a community in which the factory or the immigrant was unknown. Immigration and industrialization were major factors in the society before 1880, and yet the occupational achievements of the foreign-born group present between 1870 and 1880 were still much higher than in Newburyport. Nor can it be argued that South Bend's immigrant population was more static. The rate of transiency was as high there as in cities elsewhere (see table 3–4).

The answer seems to be not in the relative size of the city or the stability of its population, but rather in the qualifications of those who came and the stage of economic growth of the city when they arrived. It is in relation to these two factors of who came and when that South Bend seems to differ from the other cities that have been studied.

In Newburyport and Boston the immigrant population was heavily Irish. In South Bend, however, greater ethnic diversity prevailed, and the Irish were never more than a minority. Before the 1870s when the Poles began to arrive in large numbers, South Bend's dominant ethnic group was the Germans (table 3–2). Between 1850 and 1880 most of the German workers who passed through the city pursued a calling in which they worked with their hands. Even so they were never concentrated in a single manual occupation, nor were they clustered

in the lowest category. More often they were dispersed among
the carpenters, brickmasons, cabinetmakers, and blacksmiths,
as well as in semiskilled positions as butchers or sawyers and
later as factory operatives. Only in the first census, 1850, was
the largest proportion of Germans employed as unskilled laborers. In 1860 and 1870 the skilled craftsmen exceeded in
number the workers in any other category. Even in 1880, when
abundant factory jobs were available, the German workers
were employed as craftsmen as frequently as they were in
industrial positions (Appendix, table A-2). In this respect
South Bend was similar to Milwaukee and other midwestern
cities in the mid-nineteenth century.[20]

The German immigrants were also successful in entering
middle-class occupations, more so than any other ethnic group
except the English. In 1850 one in four held nonmanual jobs,
usually as small businessmen, and a few were lawyers and
physicians. The city's changing economy had caused a slight
downward slide in occupational opportunities by 1880, but out
of five Germans one was still among the business and professional classes.

If the prospects for employment were good for the German who was newly arrived in the city, they were even better
for those who stayed on for more than one census decade. Although the rate of turnover among German immigrants was
quite high, those who persisted in the community usually
prospered. The occupational status of every census group continued to be quite high. The number of Germans recorded in
the 1850 census who persisted through the following three decades was small and might be dismissed as insufficient for gen-
eralization. But as the number of workers in the 1860 and 1870
groups increased, the pattern did not change. Half or more of
those present in 1860 had attained white-collar positions by
1870 or 1880.

The best opportunities for the Germans who stayed were
as businessmen or small proprietors. Like their brethren in
New York City and Poughkeepsie, the Germans did well in
food and clothing businesses.[21] Typical was the case of the

Livingston brothers. Myer Livingston was the owner of a modest dry goods business in 1860, and during the next twenty years he made his store at 58 Washington Street one of the leading establishments of the city.[22] His brother Moses followed his example by leaving his small butcher shop to open his own retail clothing store.

The success of German residents like the Livingston brothers was affected both by the fact that they started high in the occupational scale and either maintained their positions as the city grew or even moved upward. Among the members of the 1850 and 1860 census groups who were present for one full decade there was only one case of downward mobility. Fifty per cent of the 1850 group and 38 per cent of the 1860 group had improved their occupational standing after ten years. Even between 1870 and 1880, when the city was experiencing the impact of industrialization, the number of Germans who were upwardly mobile was still greater than those who slid downward into semiskilled factory jobs. Whether they were present for more than one decade seems to have made little difference. The rate of upward mobility and the level of occupational status attained was about the same for those who stayed two decades and those who remained for only one.

Perhaps the Germans were more successful than many of the ethnic groups in eastern seaport cities because those who settled in South Bend had already begun to adjust to American society before they reached the city. Seldom were the German immigrants in South Bend fresh off the ships from Europe. The Hanauer family clearly illustrates this fact. Abram Hanauer, a Bavarian, settled in South Bend some time in the 1860s and remained at least until 1880. In 1870 he reported property valued at thirty-five thousand dollars and was one of the principal dry goods merchants in the city. The oldest of his four children was eighteen years old, and all had been born in Ohio or Indiana. The move to South Bend was at least the third for the family within the United States, and Abram Hanauer had already acquired a stock of capital and business experience before he reached South Bend. Moreover, the father was able to transfer some of the advantages he had to his sons, both of whom began their careers as clerks in white-collar positions.

The Germans enjoyed the advantages of having acquired some skills and perhaps of even having accumulated some capital before they came to South Bend, and they also benefited from the fact that the largest number of immigrants in the city before 1880 were Germans. Oscar Handlin has observed that those newcomers who drew support from their fellow countrymen had the best chance of succeeding as petty merchants.[23] German immigrants who owned small grocery stores and saloons in South Bend met the needs of the predominant ethnic group. Thus the Germans had the advantage of drawing upon the support of their fellow countrymen, an advantage that was less available to smaller groups such as the Irish.

The English, too, had advantages that other ethnic groups in South Bend did not enjoy: language and culture rather than numbers. Certainly the work of Rowland Berthoff leads us to expect that English immigrants were more successful in competing for jobs than other newcomers, but what is mildly surprising is that the English did not do exceptionally well in South Bend.[24] In 1850, 60 per cent of the gainfully employed English immigrants were in nonmanual positions, usually as small businessmen and occasionally in the professions. Ten years later, however, only one out of four was still employed in a white-collar job, and the proportion did not increase in the following decades. By 1880 four-fifths of the English-born workers were in manual occupations, nearly half being among the semiskilled (Appendix, table A-2). Although the English usually had the smallest proportion of unskilled laborers, they did not start as high in the occupational scale as might be expected. Perhaps the explanation lies in the occupational success that the English found in cities to the east. Robert Ernst found that at least 8 per cent of New York's English-born immigrants in 1855 were professionals—a percentage higher than that of any other foreign-born group.[25] Since most of South Bend's English immigrants first passed through New York and Pennsylvania, it may well be that those who found occupational opportunities in eastern cities simply did not move on to the Midwest. Nor was the successful Englishman encouraged to move west because of ethnic prejudice, which other groups like the Irish or sometimes even the Germans faced in urban centers along the Atlantic coast. Those English immigrants who came to South Bend may not have been as well prepared to compete for jobs as their more successful brethren who remained in the eastern cities. Since the census schedules provide no information on these immigrants before they appeared in South Bend, however, this must remain a hypothesis.

For immigrants from England, Scotland, and Wales who were persistent in South Bend for more than one census, the record is more explicit. The persistence rate was between 26 and 30 per cent for those who stayed one decade and about half that for those who remained longer (see table 3–4). In most cases residential stability was commensurate with high occupational achievement. In only one decade did the proportion of English wage earners in nonmanual positions fall below 50 per cent. In the 1870s 46 per cent of the English who remained were white-collar workers. Of the rest, 31 per cent were concentrated in semiskilled occupations, usually in wagon shops and foundries. Likewise this was the only decade in which any instances of downward mobility occurred.

Thus for the two most prominent ethnic groups in South Bend, the Germans and the English, residential stability was normally a reflection of occupational success. Both groups started higher in the occupational structure than immigrants of other origins, and both Englishmen and Germans experienced a moderate amount of upward mobility during the first generation. Industrialization did not block the path of these foreign-born in their search for occupational improvement, but it did at least reduce the chances of some for upward mobility.

Much attention has been given to the trials of the Irish in industrial cities. The picture that Oscar Handlin draws of Boston's Irish in the mid-nineteenth century is appropriate for many eastern cities, including Newburyport:

The mass of Irishmen continued to occupy the low places in society they had earlier held. Their wives and daughters performed most of the city's domestic service; and men and boys of Irish ancestry constituted the bulk of unskilled workers. The censuses of 1870 and 1880 still found them two-thirds of the laborers and the *Pilot* estimated that 60 per cent of the group in 1877 still occupied that rank.[26]

But this portrait is suitable for South Bend only in the earlier years, before industry prevailed. Up to the decade of the seventies, one-half to two-thirds of the Irish workers were employed as unskilled common laborers. The census of 1880, however, reported that only one out of every four males born in Ireland was at the lowest occupational level. The majority, 68 per cent, were skilled workers or factory operatives. Eight per cent had even managed to find places among the professionals or small business men (Appendix, table A-2).

If the overall occupational achievement of the Irish in South Bend was higher than in the eastern industrial cities, the reason lies in both the opportunities available in the city and the qualifications of the immigrants who came. Historians and contemporaries observed that only the Irish with sufficient health, energy, ambition, and capital moved to the interior cities where their labor was in demand. The majority, having neither the capital nor personal resources to move on, were immobilized in or near the ports of debarkation.[27] Geographical mobility in the case of the Irish was closely related to occupational mobility. Those who had the resources to reach the growing industrial cities of the Middle West stood a better chance of improving their occupational status than those who remained in Boston or New York, where competition was more difficult and prejudice more intense.

In fact, the lack of geographical mobility was in a puzzling way a limitation even on the Irish who stayed in South Bend. Unlike any other ethnic group, the Irish who remained in South Bend failed to improve their position after ten or twenty years. Arthur Burns is typical: in 1860, at a relatively young age of thirty, he was employed as a common laborer; ten years later he was still in the lowest occupational category. In 1880 when only 23 per cent of all Irish wage earners were common laborers, twice that proportion of those who were residents of the city from 1870 to 1880 were in the unskilled class. While new arrivals increasingly took better-paying jobs in the factories, the older Irish residents continued to work as gardeners, liverymen, or untrained day laborers. Stability or residence seems to have had little or no effect in improving the occupational status of the Irish, although it had done so in every other ethnic group.

For the Canadian, Polish, and Other European ethnic groups, residential stability generally resulted in increasing occupational status. Whether new arrivals or residents for at least ten years, the Canadians, Poles, Belgians, Swedes, and others usually worked with their hands; but the longer these foreign-born lived in the city, the better were their chances of becoming skilled craftsmen. Twenty-three per cent of all male wage earners classified as Other European were skilled workers in 1880; but of those who were persistent from 1870 to 1880, 57 per cent were skilled. The patterns of intragenerational mobility among these smaller ethnic groups in South Bend, however, are difficult to measure, since the number of workers who remained from one census to the next was quite small.

The magnitude of occupational mobility in mid-nineteenth-century South Bend can be measured not only for the first generation, but for their sons as well. It has been an accepted belief that the native-born of immigrant families achieved higher occupational and social status than their foreign-born parents, but it is not entirely clear how much they improved their positions or what avenues of mobility they followed.

A comparison of the occupations of the two generations suggests that the native-born sons were consistently better off than their fathers. Table 5–3 provides detailed information. In every census decade the sons were more often employed in the white-collar class than the first generation had been. Like their fathers they found entry into nonmanual jobs easiest in

1850 when the city was quite small and still dependent upon commerce. The number of employed native-born sons of immigrant families was not large in 1850—only fifteen—but by 1880, when there were over five hundred, they still found more

Table 5-3

OCCUPATIONS OF FIRST AND SECOND GENERATION IMMIGRANTS, SOUTH BEND: 1850–80
(In Percentages)

Occupation	1850		1860		1870		1880	
	Foreign-born	Native-born	Foreign-born	Native-born	Foreign-born	Native-born	Foreign-born	Native-born
Professional	6%	13%	2%	2%	2%	4%	1%	2%
Proprietors, managers, officials	3	13	4	10	5	9	3	4
Semiprofessional	—	—	—	—	—	—	—	1
Clerical and sales	3	7	4	7	2	9	2	12
Petty proprietors, managers, officials	26	20	9	12	6	2	4	3
Skilled	28	33	28	44	36	33	21	25
Semiskilled service	10	7	25	—	21	26	57	37
Unskilled, menial service	25	7	28	24	28	16	12	16

Source: Manuscript federal census, 1850, 1860, 1870, 1880.

opportunities than their fathers as clerks, businessmen, and even professionals. The evidence is clear, however, that the chance of entering a white-collar job was shrinking as the city grew and industrialization increased. In the thirty-year period after 1850 the proportion declined from one in two to one in five. As the city increased in size, fewer of the second generation were able to become owners of their own shops and small businesses, and more were employed as clerks and salesmen. A corresponding decline in the proportion of businessmen among the first generation suggests that although some sons became clerks in their fathers' stores, the majority were employed in the shops and business houses of native Americans. By 1880 the best chance for entrance into the white-collar class was clearly through employment as a clerk in one of the growing number of grocery, hardware, and clothing stores.

The effects of urbanization and industrialization are also evident in the number of second generation who followed manual callings. The number who took jobs as physical laborers had increased by 1860, but most of these were skilled laborers. They worked as blacksmiths or in the construction trades as carpenters, brickmasons, or cabinetmakers. Out of every four, one lacked the skill or the opportunity to become a craftsman and was faced with beginning his career as a common laborer. Less than 1 per cent were employed in semiskilled and service occupations. But industrial expansion following the Civil War brought an increasing concentration of the second generation in the semiskilled class. In 1870 one in four was semiskilled, and ten years later more than one-third of the native-born sons of immigrant families were working in the wagon shops, foundries, and sewing machine factories. Correspondingly, there was a reduction in the proportion who followed skilled trades or worked as common laborers. Even with the concentration in semiskilled factory jobs, however, the native-born sons were still more widely distributed throughout the occupational scale than their foreign-born fathers, and they were markedly more successful in entering white-collar positions. Twenty-two per cent of the sons had escaped the manual labor class by 1880, but only one in ten of the first generation foreign-born wore white collars (table 5–3).

This encouraging picture of the occupational achievement of second generation workers is reinforced when one considers the relative ages of the two generations. Most of the sons were young men in their late teens or early twenties who were in their first occupations when the census was taken. That half or more of these inexperienced young men in any census year began work in skilled or nonmanual callings suggests that occupational opportunities were more open to the second generation than they had been to the foreign-born.

Furthermore the persistence rates among the native-born wage earners from immigrant families indicate increased employment opportunities, although not always at the white-collar level. The ratio of persistence rose from 27 per cent between 1850 and 1860 to a stable rate of 53 per cent in the 1870s (table 3–4). The city's economic expansion following the Civil War is reflected in the fact that 43 per cent of the second generation workers remained for twenty years from 1860 to 1880. For every census group the native-born sons were approximately twice as likely to remain residentially stable as their immigrant fathers. Seldom did these younger workers who stayed fall from the positions on the occupational ladder where they had begun. There were no cases of downward mobility before 1880, and of the 102 persistent workers present in this last census only 5 per cent had dropped down from the occupation they held ten years earlier. Three times as many of the first generation workers were downwardly mobile in the same decade.[28]

Whether or not mobility was transferable from father to son is not entirely clear. Two in every three of the second generation who stayed for one census decade were able to begin their careers at a level the same as or higher than their fathers. This may, however, be merely a reflection of the overall increase in jobs available in the post–Civil War period. If it was possible to transfer occupational status, to do so was most difficult in families where the father had achieved a white-collar position. Between 1870 and 1880 only 47 per cent of the foreign-born in the business and professional classes had sons who began their careers in a nonmanual calling. Nevertheless, the second generation eventually rose to and maintained higher occupational status than their fathers.

Greater job stability for the sons was evident not only in their level of achievement, but also in their rate of unemployment. In 1880 only 11 per cent of the second generation wage earners had been unemployed at some time during the previous year, whereas 14 per cent of the foreign-born had been idle. This difference may have been greater than the statistics reveal, since some of the younger generation voluntarily took time off to attend school for a few months.

There is no doubt that the second generation of immigrants benefited immeasurably from growing up in the United States and attending American schools. The degree of their Americanization cannot be accurately determined, but their greater literacy in English helps to explain why they found business and professional positions more accessible. Illiteracy for foreign-born wage earners ranged between 8 and 16 per cent, but that of the native-born dropped from a high of 7 per cent in 1870 to only 5 per cent in 1880. More at home with the language and society of the United States than their fathers had been, the sons enjoyed greater access to middle-class occupations in South Bend.

Occupational mobility, however, is not the only index of social and economic progress among ethnic groups. Ownership of real estate and personal property is also recorded in the manuscript federal census. This type of information is of limited value, however, because it is incomplete and inaccurate. Only real estate was recorded in 1850, and no property information at all was collected in 1880. Even in 1860 and 1870, when real and personal property were recorded by the census enumerators, the information is not completely reliable. Some individuals might have withheld property information from the enumerators out of fear that they would be taxed, and others might have exaggerated the size of their holdings. Recognizing these limitations, one may use the property information as a rough estimate of the size of property holdings for each of the ethnic and occupational groups.

Since the Germans were one of the most upwardly mobile
groups in regard to occupation, it is hardly surprising that
they were among the largest property holders (see table 5–4
and Appendix, table A-3). They were businessmen and
skilled craftsmen and invested in real estate as both home
owners and speculators. In 1880, for example, Myer Livingston, John Lederer, Kasper Rockstroh, and Andrew Russworm,
all Germans, had just built or were building new business
houses at the center of the city along Main and Washington
streets. Christopher Kunstman, another Bavarian, listed fifteen thousand dollars in real estate in 1870, and a city map
of 1875 shows extensive holdings belonging to him in the First
Ward.[29]

Table 5–4
IMMIGRANT PROPERTY OWNERSHIP, SOUTH BEND: 1850–70

Place of Birth	Median Value of Personal Property			Median Value of Real Estate			Number of Cases		
	1850	1860	1870	1850	1860	1870	1850	1860	1870
Native-born of immigrant family	Not available	$149	$816	$700	$1,166	$1,749	4	19	33
British American and English		183	359	949	524	1,500	9	26	42
Irish		109	170	500	342	1,479	1	34	47
German		124	504	833	649	2,213	9	86	136
Other European		183	449	2,000	700	2,500	1	21	14

Source: Manuscript federal census, 1850, 1860, 1870.

Most German immigrants were not so wealthy as Kunstman. For the majority the real estate information in the
census reports probably represents the value of a family house
and lot and perhaps a place of business. Even so the Germans

still appear to have been prosperous. The value of the majority of the houses built in South Bend in 1869 ranged between $500 and $1,500.[30] In the following year the median value of real estate owned by German immigrants was $2,213. This median value represents no small part of the German residents. Out of 297 male wage earners, 136 (46 per cent) owned real estate. Even in 1850, when the Germans as a group were new to the city, 29 per cent owned real estate. This is in striking contrast to the 9 per cent of Newburyport's unskilled laborers who owned real property in the same year.[31]

The extent of property ownership by South Bend's German population appears less exceptional, however, when compared with that of other groups in the city. The English, Canadians, French, Belgians, and Swedes were all able to accumulate real estate and savings nearly equal to that of the Germans. In fact in 1870 the highest median value of real estate was that of immigrants in the classification Other European. The Irish owned the least property, but even their real estate holdings were almost fifteen hundred dollars per individual owner by 1870 (table 5–4).

Nevertheless, although the size of property ownership varied somewhat among different ethnic groups, the percentage of wage earners who possessed some property was generally uniform for all census years. Native-born sons of immigrant families made up the smallest proportion of property owners in 1870, and this is probably the result of the large number of young men who were employed in their first occupations and had not yet accumulated any property.

When property ownership is examined on the basis of occupation, the foreign-born laborers of South Bend show evidence of growing prosperity (table 5–5). For workers in all categories the median amount of real estate multiplied several times between 1850 and 1870. Those in the professions, business, and management positions owned real estate worth $5,800 or more by 1870. Since South Bend was expanding in population and industry, this was perhaps to be expected. But the median value of real estate owned by blue-collar workers also underwent a significant increase. Holdings of skilled workers nearly tripled to more than $2,200 by 1870, and the proportional growth of real estate holdings among unskilled workers was even larger. Moreover, not only did the median

Table 5-5

REAL ESTATE OF IMMIGRANT OCCUPATIONAL GROUPS, SOUTH BEND: 1850-70

	1850			1860			1870		
Occupational Class	Median	Number	% with Property	Median	Number	% with Property	Median	Number	% with Property
Professional	$1,249	3	50%	$5,750	2	29%	$6,249	6	25%
Proprietors, managers, officials	—	—	—	1,625	11	61	5,892	29	58
Semiprofessional	—	—	—	—	—	—	—	—	—
Clerical and sales	—	—	—	—	—	—	1,374	5	17
Petty proprietors, managers, officials	574	7	33	1,649	19	54	5,499	26	58
Skilled	849	8	33	609	58	51	2,211	99	32
Semiskilled and service	—	—	—	949	15	17	1,713	34	18
Unskilled and menial service	400	4	22	336	48	45	1,482	59	26

Source: Manuscript federal census, 1850, 1860, 1870.

value of real estate owned by South Bend's laboring class exceed that of other industrial cities, but the proportion of workers who possessed property was greater than that of the workers in Poughkeepsie or Newburyport.[32] As South Bend developed into a prospering and expanding city after the mid-century, the immigrants and their children benefited in jobs and savings.

The opportunity to accumulate property is especially evident for those immigrant families who settled in South Bend for ten years or more. In 1850 and 1860 one-half of the wage earners who remained for a decade owned property. This was a higher proportion of property ownership than among the immigrants who were more transient, even though the median size of the holdings was approximately the same (table 5–6). After ten years, however, two-thirds of the persistent workers owned property in amounts that were larger than those of other immigrants. Not only were those who owned property more inclined to stay in South Bend, but their stability greatly increased their chances of accumulating more in savings and real estate.

The influence of property, which appears strong among the 1850 and 1860 groups who persisted, however, declined noticeably by 1870. Only 31 per cent of the immigrant workers who stayed from 1870 to 1880 were property owners. Similarly, 39 per cent who remained in South Bend for two decades from 1860 to 1880 reported property in the census. These were the same years in which South Bend's industrial expansion began and the proportion of immigrants in nonmanual occupations declined (table 5–3). And yet this apparent narrowing of opportunities in jobs and savings did not result in reduced persistence: in fact, the overall persistence rate rose from 18 per cent in the 1850s to 26 per cent between 1870 and 1880 (table 3–4).

To explain this inverse relation between overall persistence rates and the occupational-economic opportunities available, it is necessary to reemphasize the changing nature of South Bend's immigrant population. Although industrialization had only a slight effect on the status of older immigrant groups —like the Germans—who were present in considerable numbers before the 1870s, the creation of new factory jobs clearly improved the opportunities of later immigrants—like the Poles —who came directly from Europe in large numbers after 1870.

Table 5-6

PROPERTY OWNERSHIP AND PERSISTENCE, SOUTH BEND: 1850–70

	1850					1860					1870				
	Number of Workers	Number of Property Owners	% Who Are Property Owners	Median Value of Real Estate	Median Value of Personal Property	Number of Workers	Number of Property Owners	% Who Are Property Owners	Median Value of Real Estate	Median Value of Personal Property	Number of Workers	Number of Property Owners	% Who Are Property Owners	Median Value of Real Estate	Median Value of Personal Property
All immigrant workers	84	24	28%	$824	Not available	385	182	47%	$586	$142	875	259	30%	$1,826	$ 449
1850–60 persistence group	15	8	53	840	Not available	15	10	67	850	300					
1860–70 persistence group						62	33	53	900	184	62	40	65	5,000	1,166
1870–80 persistence group											228	70	31	3,461	568
1860–80 persistence group						59	23	39	828	200	59	29	49	7,500	1,748

Source: Manuscript federal census, 1850, 1860, 1870, 1880.

Without the opening up of jobs in new industries many of these later immigrants would have had to accept positions as unskilled laborers. Thus for the majority of South Bend's immigrants after 1870 industrialization actually offered the means for limited upward mobility, and many were encouraged to stay in the city.

Although the success of James Oliver was unique among the thousands of immigrants who passed through or settled in South Bend in the years between 1850 and 1880, there were many others who found opportunities for work and economic progress in this midwestern city. The German or English craftsmen and businessmen who arrived by mid-century and stayed on to participate in the city's growth and industrial expansion experienced occupational and economic mobility that their brethren in the older industrial cities to the east found more difficult to achieve. Likewise they saw their sons continue the progress, even if the advancement was moderate. In the case of newer immigrants like the Poles, the industries of South Bend provided an abundance of jobs and stability that signified an improvement over their former status in Europe.

Industrialization in South Bend led to a greater concentration of immigrants in semiskilled positions, but it by no means blocked the routes of occupational and economic mobility. Those who persisted were able to inch upward in the occupational scale, perhaps not as dramatically as men like Oliver or Knoblock, but at least toward the top of the manual classes and sometimes even into the ranks of the white-collar workers. Nor was the rapid growth of foreign immigration detrimental to the urban expansion of South Bend. Without the thousands of workers eager for jobs in the new factories, South Bend might have languished in the shadow of Chicago. In the environment of a new city, where change was rapid and residential and class lines were still forming, the immigrants could contribute not only their labor but also their ideas, their talents, and even their leadership.

6

PATTERNS OF
IMMIGRANT LEADERSHIP

The role of the immigrant in South Bend's urban growth was not confined to that of factory worker or shopkeeper. As the city grew and the life of its inhabitants became more urban, some individuals from the ranks of the foreign-born rose to positions of influence and authority. When schools and churches were established, literary and social organizations founded, and political offices filled, there were men of foreign birth on hand to share in the decisions that shaped the urban community. These were men whose reputation and influence reached beyond the local ethnic neighborhoods and social clubs to the larger society of the city. The attempt to find out who these community leaders were and why they rose above their fellow immigrants reveals not only the characteristics and career patterns of some of the most mobile individuals, but also provides insight into the social life and organization of South Bend's immigrants.

Leadership implies that an individual possesses some personal quality, some notable talent, or some rare ambition that enables him to win the recognition of his associates. Unfortunately, the information gathered from census reports, city directories, newspapers, or brief biographical sketches in county histories reveals little clear knowledge about the personalities of individuals. Despite this limitation, however, it is still possible to determine who the leaders were by establishing a specific set of criteria against which certain known facts may be measured.

The first criterion for determining leadership is election and reelection to local city and county offices or election to a state office. A second criterion is prominence in social organizations. For the foreign-born and their children in South Bend this would include a position of importance in the Masons, Odd Fellows, Turnverein, or the various churches and schools. Third is the achievement of some notable success within a particular occupation. For example, James Oliver, who seems to have held no formal positions in either politics or social organizations, was, nevertheless, respected as one of the leading manufacturers and businessmen in the city. Oliver's business activities were always noted and applauded by newspaper editors eager to boost South Bend's growth. In most cases, however, individuals who were successful within their profession or job were usually chosen to be leaders of social and political groups as well. The fourth test for leadership is frequent mention of an individual in the local press. This last criterion is more subjective than the other three in that it depends upon the judgment of the researcher and his familiarity with the press. It is not, however, any less valuable in determining leadership. Some flexibility must be retained in discerning who the actual leaders were, for as Oscar Handlin has pointed out, leadership in the nineteenth-century city was not always synonymous with election to political office.[1] Newspaper accounts of important social and civic activities as well as the gossip columns provide the best source for discovering those leaders whose names do not appear in the local election records or in the lists of officers for community organizations.

Application of these tests to the immigrant population of South Bend reveals that there were twenty-eight individuals who qualify as leaders during the period from 1850 to 1880. No individual was classified as a leader who did not meet at least two of the four requirements. Some, for example, were elected to offices within their social clubs but had no apparent influence in the larger community. They were not elected to any political office nor were they mentioned with any consistency in the press. Only those who showed evidence of being influential in more than one sphere—in politics as well as in business for example, or in manufacturing as well as in the Masons—were selected as active leaders.

Of the twenty-eight leaders, twenty-one were first generation immigrants and seven were the sons of immigrant parents. Among the foreign-born the most striking characteristic is that a majority were from non-English-speaking countries. No fewer than eleven of the twenty-one leaders who were born outside the United States were from the German states of Bavaria, Hesse, and Prussia. Bavaria produced the largest number—six—of German-American leaders. England contributed one more than did Bavaria, but the total from English-speaking countries (including Scotland and Canada) was only nine.[2] None of the leaders was born in Ireland. The other foreign-born leader, Nicholas Tanski, was from Prussian Poland. The national origins of those leaders who were native-born but had at least one foreign-born parent differed only slightly: four had parents from English-speaking nations, principally Ireland, and three were descendants of French or German parents.

The national origins of the immigrant leaders in South Bend are of particular interest when compared to the conclusions of Merle Curti in regard to Trempealeau County, Wisconsin. Curti found that although some community leaders came from Canada or England before 1860, none were from non-English-speaking countries. In South Bend, however, six of the fifteen leaders who arrived before 1860 were German. Of the remaining nine, seven were from English nations and two were native-born, with parents from France and Prussia. After the Civil War decade Trempealeau County and South Bend became more alike in their patterns of immigrant leadership, each with about half the leaders coming from non-English-speaking countries.[3]

In other characteristics of leadership there was little difference between the rural frontier of Wisconsin and the urban frontier of South Bend. Before 1860 it was not uncommon for a man under thirty to become a leader in the community. After that time, however, as the society developed and population increased, the average age of the leaders became progressively older.[4] The age of the immigrant leaders in South Bend increased from an average of only thirty years in 1860 to almost fifty by 1880.

The increased average age of the leaders as the city grew in size was in part affected by their residential stability. Nineteen of the twenty-eight leaders were present by the beginning of the Civil War and nearly all of them stayed on through 1880. In a city with a high population turnover, such permanence undoubtedly enhanced their opportunities for assuming positions of authority. The average length of residence for the twenty-eight leaders was 14.4 years. Although this figure represents less than half of the thirty years between 1850 and 1880, it is more meaningful if certain considerations are kept in mind. Of the twenty-eight leaders, twenty-four were still residents of South Bend in 1880. How many of these twenty-four continued to live there after 1880 is not definitely known since the census records for 1890 are not available. Those who came in the late 1860s may have stayed after 1880 and have been more permanent than the 14.4 figure suggests. Moreover, the average length of residence is influenced by the fact that it is based primarily on decennial reports: an immigrant who came in 1861 would not appear in the census until 1870. Whenever possible the city directories, newspapers, and biographies were used to supplement the census information, but even these sources have some limitations. John Haggerty, for example, does not appear in the census records until 1870, but he was elected city clerk in 1866.[5] How long he was present before being elected to public office is not known, since the city directories began to appear only after 1867.

More certain is where the immigrant leaders lived. If one walked northward from the central business area along the board sidewalks of Main Street, he would pass the spacious homes of native-born leaders like Colonel Norman Eddy and John M. Studebaker. Turning west along Market it would be only a few blocks before one reached the house of South Bend's most famous politician, Schuyler Colfax. It was along these streets and in the surrounding neighborhoods of the First and Second wards that the immigrant leaders lived. Only three lived outside this area in 1870, and only six lived in the other wards of the city in 1880.

The location of the homes of South Bend's most prominent immigrant families suggests not only that they lived in the same neighborhoods as the city's native-born elite, but also reveals something about their occupational characteristics. Since most of them lived within a short walk from the center of the city, it is not surprising to find that for the most part they were businessmen and professionals. Almost two-thirds of the occupations listed by the leaders between 1850 and 1880 were of the white-collar class (compare with table 5–1). Their high rate of occupational mobility is demonstrated by the fact that eight of the thirteen who originally held manual labor jobs later moved up into the nonmanual class. Manufacturers, retail and wholesale merchants, lawyers, physicians, and publishers made up the majority of this elite group. Those from English origins, like Robert Harris, a physician, were most successful in reaching positions of leadership from professional occupations, whereas German-Americans, like the Livingston brothers, were most often from the ranks of the businessmen. The career patterns of the second generation leaders were similar.

High social and occupational status was closely related to the wealth of the ethnic leaders. The median value of real estate and personal property owned by the leaders in 1860 and 1870 was substantially higher than that of other immigrants. The median value of their real estate increased from $1,249 in 1860 to $3,749 in 1870 while their personal assets increased from $449 to $2,415 (compare with table 5–4). There were several manufacturers and businessmen like Joseph Warden, who reported property valued at more than $10,000. James Oliver was the wealthiest, with more than $300,000, most of which was stock in his plow factory.[6]

In their jobs, in their wealth, in the location of their homes, and in their persistence in the community, these men stood out among the ethnic population of South Bend. Undoubtedly they expected to pass on many of these advantages to their children. Since they were usually men of some economic stability and also because they were probably more aware of the value of education, they were more likely to send their children to school and to keep them there for a longer time. For most immigrant families in South Bend the number of children who actually attended school was never large, often falling well below 50 per cent. But among the school-age children of the leaders, 94 per cent attended school between 1850 and 1880. The benefit of education coupled with their fathers' high social and occupational mobility usually enabled the children of South Bend's ethnic leaders to maintain positions in the white-collar class. Joseph Oliver, for example, became his father's secretary and accountant, and Otto Knoblock started his career as the secretary for the Miller-Knoblock Electric Company.[7]

The analysis of common characteristics of the most prominent immigrants reveals their statistical profile, and a few typical examples will further illustrate their career patterns. Henry Ginz was a man with considerable political experience by the time he arrived in South Bend in 1869 at the age of thirty-nine. A cabinetmaker in Alzey, Hesse-Darmstadt, he took part in the rebellion of 1849 and later escaped to Switzerland. Eventually pardoned, he returned to his native town, though his stay there was only temporary. By 1854, either by his own choice or because of pressure from his political adversaries, he once again left Germany and came to America. Like many other German immigrants he was, in his early years in the United States, highly mobile geographically, practicing his trade as a cabinetmaker in New York, then later in La Porte County (Indiana) and Indianapolis. When he moved to South Bend in 1869, he changed occupations to become a grocer and baker before finally buying a share in J. C. Knoblock's flour mill.[8] By South Bend's standards he was not wealthy, but he did own fifteen hundred dollars worth of real estate and two thousand dollars in other personal assets.

Change of location and occupation, however, did not cause Ginz to lose those interests and talents which had made him politically active as a young man in Germany. Within two years he was elected to office in the local Turnverein, and his reputation spread throughout the city and county.[9] He used his position as a leader of the city's most important German organization to develop his influence in the local Democratic party, for by 1878 he was elected over Judge William Stanfield as representative to the state legislature.[10] His residence at 70 Market Street may not have been as impressive as that of his close neighbor Schuyler Colfax, but he was clearly one of South Bend's most influential politicians.

The career of George W. Matthews, an English immigrant, was neither as varied nor as dramatic as that of Henry Ginz.[11] A lawyer by profession, Matthews became a resident of South Bend some time before 1860, when he was still in his twenties, and quickly settled into a pattern of being elected and reelected to local office. His frequent selection as either trustee or clerk of the town put him in a good position to become the city's first treasurer in 1865, after incorporation was approved by the voters. Being a Republican in the 1860s was certainly no disadvantage to Matthews, and apparently he had some personal popularity, for in 1867 he defeated his opponent for county clerk by a vote of 1,014 to 68. He held on to office through the politically uncertain years of 1873 and 1874 and was removed only when the Democrats swept all of the offices in 1875.[12]

The last example of ethnic leadership is brief but meaningful. Nicholas Tanski at thirty-three was the youngest of the leaders in 1880 and the only one from Polish Prussia. According to the ages and birthplaces of his children he migrated to South Bend from Prussia sometime between 1877 and 1880. He listed his occupation as teacher but also acted as "notary public, steamship passenger agent, collection agent, insurance and real estate dealer, mediator of small problems arising between Poles and the rest of the community, and close observer of the polls."[13] In other words, he was South Bend's first Polish political boss. His election on the Democratic ticket as justice of the peace in 1880 would not be justification in itself to qualify him as a leader, but clearly his influence in the community and the Democratic party went beyond that of any formal office.

Most of the characteristics of South Bend's twenty-eight ethnic leaders require little additional explanation. It is not uncommon for the leaders of any group to be those with the better jobs, to possess more capital resources, or to live in the best houses. But there is one unique feature in the leadership patterns of South Bend's immigrants that does require elaboration. Merle Curti discovered no leaders in Trempealeau County before 1860 who came from non-English-speaking countries. In South Bend, however, nearly half of the foreign-born leaders before and after 1860 came from Germany. Since both of these communities contained a diversity of ethnic groups, why were the Germans of South Bend so much more successful in achieving positions of leadership than were the non-English-speaking immigrants of Trempealeau County?

In the records and newspapers of the city, the principal factor that seems to explain the differences in the leadership patterns is the participation of South Bend's German-Americans in community social activities and in the development of voluntary associations. Even in the early years of South Bend, before the number of foreign-born residents was very large, the immigrants, particularly the Germans, led active social lives. When the community was small and close contact frequent, the foreign-born took part in the street life, celebrations, and various social entertainments without suffering from any apparent discrimination. More importantly, as the number of foreign newcomers increased, they began to establish social clubs and associations out of which many of the ethnic leaders later emerged. In other words, the immigrants in South Bend established social contacts with the native-born majority more quickly and with less difficulty than did the immigrants in the rural frontier society of Trempealeau County. The development of an active social life accelerated the adjustment of immigrants to their American environment and boosted the more talented among them into positions of authority.

Because it went unrecorded, much of the character and flavor of immigrant social life in South Bend cannot be recaptured. In the small town of the 1850s, where the shops and homes of the foreign-born were interspersed with those of the native American, there must have been daily contact between those of different nationalities. Neighbor met neighbor, and the process of acceptance and adjustment between native and foreign-born followed a simple and personal course. It was not long, however, before this growing community on the urban frontier began to develop a more formal social life. The ethnic group that contributed the most to the social activities of the community was the Germans. There were lectures, concerts, plays, and holiday celebrations in which the whole community, including the foreign-born, participated. But there were also a number of social entertainments in which the Germans took the initiative. City residents who were not satisfied with the traveling troupes of "Bohemian Glass Blowers" or Zouavian drill teams could enjoy for twenty cents the regular performances of the local German theatrical groups. The plays of the German Dramatic Society, organized in 1858, were always well attended and constantly praised by the local press. Under the dim, smoky oil lamps of Shively's Hall the Germans acted out their versions of *Uncle Tom's Cabin* and *Ten Nights in a Bar Room.* Philip Klingel's portrayal of an obese comedian may not have matched Edwin Booth's Hamlet at Good's Opera House, but the community appreciated its local German talent, and the tickets were less expensive than the three-dollar seats at Booth's performances. More important than the tastes of the audiences, however, was the fact that during the period when the urban community of South Bend was taking shape, the Germans made valuable contributions to social and cultural life, and their efforts were usually acknowledged by the approval and participation of the native-born majority.[14]

Besides the theater there were other social activities offered by the Germans. Masquerade balls and dances were always popular among them, and admission was not restricted to their own countrymen. The local press often encouraged everyone to attend, with the assurance "that it will be done up in true German style."[15] Immigrant and native dancers exchanged friendship and bruises while they danced the polka and "waltzed" to tunes like "Root Hog or Die," "Captain Jinks," "Coming through the Rye," or "My Father Was a Shoemaker" played by Elbel's Cornet Band.[16]

Only slightly more dangerous to the health was the participation of native- and foreign-born in local sports. Baseball was probably the most popular sport after its introduction to the city in 1861 by Henry Benjamin, and the number of organized teams multiplied rapidly in the years after the Civil War. The German team of Head Cheeses competed regularly with the Red Necks, Atlantics, and Clippers. On the playing fields as well as in the dance halls and theaters, native and ethnic residents had a growing sense of community.[17]

The acceptance of immigrants, especially the Germans, into the social life and entertainments of the young community was unquestionably an asset to those who were to become leaders. The informal contacts with the native-born majority meant that some men developed reputations that reached beyond their circle of friends from the old country. But the immigrant leaders of South Bend had an additional advantage in that they had the support of members in specific social organizations. Between 1850 and 1880 there were approximately twenty-eight active organizations founded in the city. Of these, six were distinctly German, and at least four others contained a number of German-Americans. The Turnverein was clearly the most important and probably the largest, but there were also active German-American chapters of the Masons and Odd Fellows.[18] The Maennerchor Society met weekly at its hall on Sycamore Street to sing the old songs of the fatherland and to offer choral concerts to the public. Hose Company Number 1, a volunteer fire company with twenty-five members, mostly German, was as important in its social functions as it was in fighting fires. The dances, Fourth of July celebrations, and parades which the company sponsored were nearly as valuable as the buckets its members wielded. Though most leaders were officers in the ethnic organizations, some held positions in the predominantly native-born societies like the Knights of Pythias.[19]

No fewer than eleven of the twelve German leaders in South Bend between 1850 and 1880 were officers in one or more of these diverse and distinctive voluntary associations. Over half of the leaders who were active in German and native clubs were elected to political office; the rest were important leaders of the business community or in some way influential outside the life of the organizations. John Klingel, for example, was one of the speakers on the platform at the Masonic celebration of Saint John's Day in 1870. In this capacity he was representing the leadership of the Germania Lodge, but his reputation and influence extended beyond that of the Masons. He was not only the first councilman for the Fourth Ward, but he also served on the Board of Education continuously from 1868 to 1881.[20]

The participation of the German-Americans in voluntary associations was an advantage to those who became community leaders in at least two ways. First of all, the social organizations helped the immigrant to become Americanized. This was true not only for Germans who belonged to predominantly native societies, but even for those in associations like the Turnverein. Although a German organization, the Turnverein itself became Americanized in its attempt to cooperate with other native organizations and to adjust to the social environment of South Bend. Those who joined such an organization as well as those who attended the theater and masquerade balls were participating in their new environment, and these activities were a part of their adjustment to an American way of life. Moreover, a second advantage of membership was that the leaders gained experience in positions of authority and support in their efforts to achieve leadership in the larger urban community. Leaders of the Turnverein could rely upon the votes of their fellow members when they sought election to the city council or county offices. As Handlin has observed, the leaders of immigrant associations had one thing in common, "that they were concerned with using their positions to make an impression in the general society."[21]

The answer, then, to the question of why immigrants from non-English-speaking countries were able to achieve positions of leadership earlier and in greater proportion to their numbers in South Bend than in Trempealeau County seems to lie in their greater participation in the social life and organizations of the community. In the rural environment of Wisconsin, geographic and social isolation tended to retard the adjustment of the non-English immigrant to American society and limit his opportunities for leadership. In fact the German-Americans of South Bend may even have possessed an advantage over their countrymen in the larger cities of the East. The immigrant faced disorganization of his social life if he lived on the isolated farm or in the overcrowded ghetto of a large city. In the congested ethnic districts of New York or Boston the immigrant might become an important figure in his local club, but only the rarest of individuals could transfer his reputation or influence to the larger society of the city. In a city the size of South Bend, however, where social and residential lines were still forming, there was neither the isolation of the rural frontier nor the fragmentation of the metropolis.

The hypothesis that participation in social organizations was the key to the success of South Bend's German-Americans in acquiring community leadership is strengthened when one compares their experiences and the experiences of those of English-speaking background. Although the total number of immigrants from English-speaking nations and Germany was nearly the same for the census years 1850–80, the Germans could claim eleven of the city's leaders and the British only nine. This small difference would not be of exceptional interest but for the fact that historians have persistently argued that those foreign-born who came from English-speaking countries usually had an easier time adjusting to American society. The experience of South Bend's ethnic leaders does not disprove the conclusion that English-speaking immigrants probably became assimilated more quickly, but it does suggest that to become a community leader the immigrant often needed something more than the ability to blend into the American society. It suggests that involvement and leadership in certain social organizations were significant factors. Of the twenty-eight organizations that were formed in South Bend before 1880, none were started or controlled by British immigrants or their descendants. Rowland Berthoff claims that the British were as enthusiastic as other immigrant groups in organizing a variety of clubs and societies, but this was clearly not true of South Bend.[22] There were no fraternal orders, no cultural or literary societies, no musical groups, and no mutual aid and benevolent associations created specifically for Englishmen, Scots, or even Irish. They joined various lodges, such as the Masons or Odd Fellows, but these organizations continued to be dominated by native Americans. Whereas the Germans set up their own organizations and promoted their own leaders into positions of responsibility in the general community, the British seem to have been absorbed quietly into the society of the native-born residents.

The only institution that immigrants from English-speaking origins may be said to have dominated was the church. But such immigrants were Irish Catholics and the associational structure of Saint Patrick's Parish was designed to keep the members separate from the community rather than to promote their integration. The Germans persuaded the city to buy German language books for the library, and they opened a "German Select School" in 1876; but the desire for separation from the community seems never to have been so strong or deliberate as among the Irish Catholics.[23]

The Poles were another numerically significant group that failed to contribute leaders to the community in proportion to its total population. Only Nicholas Tanski, a political jack-of-all-trades, could lay claim to the title of leader before 1880. Part of the Poles' failure too, like that of the British, may have been caused by a lack of participation in community organizations. They did form some voluntary associations of their own, but these remained distinctly ethnic, with little claim to influence in the rest of the urban community. The Saint Stanislaus Kostka Society and the Saint Casimir Society, both established in 1874, were sick- and death-benefit societies designed to maintain Polish Catholic unity. Three years later the desire to have their own priests and to be free of the Irish domination of Saint Patrick's led the Poles to establish their own parish. The unity of the Polish community would eventually make the Poles a significant factor in the city's politics, but before 1880 they contributed little leadership to the whole community.[24]

It would be unfair, however, to leave the impression that the Poles were solely responsible for their failure to develop leaders in the city affairs. Their attempts to maintain a Polish Catholic community and their concentration in manual occupations did not enhance their social position, but they did face some obstacles that were not of their own choosing. Their arrival in the 1870s, for example, meant that unlike earlier immigrant groups they were entering a city which, though small, had already begun to establish a distinct housing pattern. The better residential sections of the First and Second wards near the central business area had been taken up in the previous decades by native Americans and older immigrants. Consequently the Poles settled farther out in the Third and Fifth wards, where they were more physically isolated than any previous ethnic group. Added to this was the fact that as the city rapidly increased in size in the 1870s, individuals necessarily became more obscure. Newspapers that earlier had reported the most ordinary activities of individual inhabitants were now able to take notice of only the more important citizens. These normally tended to be the older residents with established reputations. The Polish immigrants who were most quickly noticed by the press were those who committed crimes.[25]

Moreover the new arrivals from Polish Prussia in the 1870s encountered prejudice and were only reluctantly accepted into the society of the city. Although the English and Germans had met no great resistance to their participation in the societies, lodges, and political life of the city, the Poles were more often considered foreigners who did not belong. The press that recommended Henry Hartwick as the Democratic candidate for sheriff in 1858 partly because of his "German accent" and in 1880 could promote Fred Lang as "an honest German" for county treasurer had few words of praise for the Poles.[26] The Poles were mocked for their style of living, for their wedding celebrations, and even for their names. In a single account of a murder trial the local editor intentionally misspelled the Polish defendant's name nine different ways.[27] Prejudice of this sort, coupled with the late arrival of the Poles, tended to limit their chances for becoming community leaders before 1880.

The analysis of immigrant leadership illustrates several significant points regarding the interaction between immigration and urbanization. The first is that the time of arrival was crucial in determining not only the ease with which the immigrant was assimilated into the urban environment, but also the extent to which the immigrant could play a leading role in shaping the development of that environment. Those, like the Germans and English, who came initially in the 1850s and 1860s, found a small commercial town not far removed from the farming frontier, one where their talents and capital were needed and where class lines and residential boundaries were still weakly defined. Where nearly everyone was a newcomer there was no stigma attached to foreign birth; consequently immigrant and native-born alike shared in the economic and social opportunities that were available. The small size of the young city facilitated the integration of the ethnic families into the community and enabled them to share in the decisions that shaped the physical and social development of South Bend. Those who came later, like the Poles, found a larger industrial city, where economic opportunities were more limited and the social structure more rigid. They were needed and invited as workers for the factories but not accepted as social equals.

From a different perspective time was also a crucial factor not only in relation to the stage of urbanization when the immigrant arrived but in how long he stayed. Certainly the German leader benefited from the persistence of the Germans as a group and from the continuity of their social organizations, but more directly an individual's chances of becoming a community leader were increased the longer he stayed. In a young community, where the population turnover was rapid, the individual who remained stable could quickly become a man of some influence and reputation.

Finally, the experience of South Bend's ethnic leaders emphasizes the importance of well-defined and active social organizations. The individual newcomer often profited from the continuity of his fellow countrymen as a group. And when this continuity was deliberately perpetuated by specific ethnic organizations such as the Turnverein, the newly arrived individual with potential for leadership possessed a ready-made base for support. A prime example is Henry Ginz, who settled in 1869 and ten years later was in the state legislature. Ethnic organizations like the Saint Stanislaus Kostka Society, of course—which promoted Polish separation—were less effective in developing leaders than those like the Germania Lodge of the Masons, which encouraged cooperation with the native-born society. As urbanization intensified and the immigrant population increased, those organizations with contacts and influence throughout the city could at least for a time counteract the tendency toward greater anonymity and social fragmentation.

7

ETHNICITY AND MOBILITY

As a city that experienced the full impact of immigration, industrialization, and rapid urban growth in the thirty years between 1850 and 1880, South Bend is representative of the major changes that were affecting much of the United States in the latter half of the nineteenth century. For many cities of the Midwest these were the years of initial expansion, when the geographic, political, economic, and social foundations were laid. Each city was unique, but all were part of a common social and economic order that underwent basic changes before the end of the century. Patterns of growth and change in South Bend were common to many other urban communities.

The interaction among these three major forces of growth in South Bend before 1880 is best understood if the city's development is considered as having two periods or stages. The first is a preindustrial period that includes those years up to and during the Civil War. From a small trading post on the banks of the Saint Joseph River, South Bend underwent modest growth as a commercial center for the surrounding farmlands of north central Indiana. The immigrants who settled there were Germans, English, Irish, and French Canadians, who opened small shops and businesses, worked as skilled carpenters and blacksmiths, or became common laborers in the town or on nearby farms.

This initial period was one of modest growth, but the second period of development, after the Civil War, was one of rapid change, characterized by a transition from commerce to industry and the influx of thousands of immigrants from Polish Prussia and other European countries. Beginning in 1867 and 1868, when waterpower was fully developed and prospering manufacturers like Oliver, Studebaker, and Singer expanded, the city quickly became one of the leading industrial and population centers of the state. Through the interaction of immigration, urbanization, and industrialization, South Bend was transformed in appearance and in internal social and economic structure.

A major factor in South Bend's whole process of urban growth before 1880 is the high rate of geographical mobility among its immigrant population. Although it was more common for successful German businessmen like the Livingston brothers or English professionals like Dr. Robert Harris to remain than for the common laborers, seldom did more than one in five of the immigrants recorded in the census lists stay in South Bend for as long as ten years between 1850 and 1870 (table 3–4). Industrialization seems to have had a slight effect upon the persistence patterns of immigrants after 1870 as more jobs for the semiskilled were available in the new manufacturing plants. Nevertheless, even during a period of dramatic industrial and economic expansion, barely one employed male immigrant in four was willing to remain in the city for a decade. As Stephan Thernstrom found in Newburyport, persistence appears to have been almost an independent variable, only slightly affected by the increase in industrialization and urban growth.[1] The second generation of immigrant families was somewhat more stable, but the persistence rate usually remained below 50 per cent, and the general impression of constant movement and change in population remains. In this respect South Bend was much like Omaha, even though

Omaha was much larger, and most immigrants were employed in commerce rather than industry.[2]

Another factor of some importance for understanding the process of urbanization in nineteenth-century cities is the level of ethnic segregation, which was low in South Bend. Many eariler studies have left the impression that ethnically segregated sections of cities were formed as a result of a conscious decision made by either the immigrants themselves, who wanted to maintain the culture of the old country, or by the older native-born residents, who did not want to mingle with the foreign-born newcomers. The evidence from South Bend, however, suggests that ethnic segregation was weak or almost nonexistent in the early years or preindustrial stage of the community.

When South Bend began to develop a more fragmented residential pattern after the Civil War, it was as much or more a result of industrialization and the changing occupational structure as it was a result of ethnicity. When the first Polish immigrants arrived, they were attracted to the Third Ward, in the southwest portion of the city, because it was there in the new factories that they found jobs, and it was there that Studebaker and Oliver had built homes for the workers. Lacking capital to become businessmen and the training to become professionals or skilled craftsmen, the Poles settled in that area of the city where their talents were most in demand and there was housing to meet their needs. Only later, after thousands of Polish workers had arrived and religious and social institutions had been founded, did the Third Ward begin to attract immigrants from Polish Prussia who were conscious of their ethnicity.[3]

Immigration and industrialization together changed the appearance and residential structure of South Bend, and they also affected the economic structure of the urban community. The changes that occurred can be viewed from two different perspectives: the impact of urban-industrial growth or the occupational mobility of immigrants and the role of the foreign-born in the economic growth of the city.

The effect of urban growth and industrialization upon immigrant work patterns is impressive if one looks at the overall occupational situation between 1850 and 1880. In 1850, 63 per cent of all foreign-born workers were employed in manual occupations, most as skilled artisans or common day laborers (table 5–3). Thirty years later, nine out of every ten male wage earners born outside the United States held blue-collar jobs, and a majority—57 per cent—were classified as semiskilled. Similarly, the second generation followed the same pattern, with blue-collar employment increasing from 47 to 78 per cent between 1850 and 1880. Here, too, the largest were semiskilled laborers in the city's manufacturing establishments.

These statistics are misleading, however, since the magnitude of the changes was not the same for all ethnic groups. While the economic characteristics of the city were changing, the sources of immigration were changing also. The Polish immigration of the seventies quickly surpassed in number that of all other groups combined. Since nearly all of these new immigrants had been attracted by the factories—77 per cent were semiskilled in 1880 (Appendix, table A-2)—their presence distorts the occupational picture of all the foreign-born. Only a minority of the Germans, Irish, or Canadians became semiskilled factory workers: a large proportion continued to earn their living as skilled craftsmen or small businessmen. Thus industrialization had the greatest impact upon new immigrant groups and only a moderate effect upon those groups that had been coming to the city over a longer period of time.

Although the proportion of immigrants in nonmanual occupations generally declined as South Bend developed, it would be misleading to conclude that this trend signified blocked mobility for the foreign-born. Not only were the position and pay of the industrial laborer often an improvement over what he had known in Europe, but the opportunities were also better than would have been available had industrialization not occurred. Since the majority of the Poles had neither the capital nor training to become businessmen or craftsmen in the

American system, without industrialization they would have had no choice but to accept the status of common laborer. Even among the older ethnic groups, such as the Irish, jobs in manufacturing sometimes represented upward occupational mobility (Appendix, table A-2). For these two groups, urbanization and industrialization encouraged upward mobility.

For those who stayed ten years or more in South Bend, the chances of improving their status were good. The opportunities for upward mobility among those in manual occupations were much better in South Bend than in Newburyport (table 5–2). Nearly a third of all the persistent foreign-born who were in blue-collar positions in 1860 held nonmanual jobs by 1870. During the following decade of industrial expansion, 13 per cent of those who initially worked with their hands achieved white-collar status, and one out of three rose to the top level of the manual class by becoming skilled craftsmen. The Germans and English who became permanent residents usually achieved a higher status than other ethnic groups. Seldom did the proportion of German and English in white-collar occupations drop below 50 per cent. Business ownership was the most frequent escape from manual labor, but some found success in the professions as lawyers, physicians, or teachers. Individuals of other ethnic backgrounds who stayed on during South Bend's transition from commerce to industry were less likely to enter the nonmanual class, but they did reach the top of the manual occupations by becoming members of a skilled trade. Only among the Irish does the relation between length of residence and upward occupational mobility appear to have been small.

The native-born sons of immigrant parents, as could have been expected, were consistently more upwardly mobile than their fathers. It was easier for them to begin in white-collar jobs—frequently as store clerks—during the city's commercial stage; but even by 1880 they were still employed twice as often as their fathers in nonmanual jobs (table 5–3). Industrialization led to an increase in the number who began their careers wearing blue collars, but the change was not significantly large.

The interaction between immigration and industrialization can also be considered in terms of the effect the foreign-born and their children had on the city's urban-industrial expansion. Obviously they provided a large part of the labor force for the new factories. The increase in immigration to South Bend, especially after the Civil War, was one of the important multipliers which stimulated urban and industrial growth. Initially there were sufficient laborers on hand for manufacturers like Studebaker and Oliver to begin production on a modest scale. As the factories grew in size, immigrants from Europe were more easily attracted to the city, coming either on their own or because they had learned of the available opportunities from family and friends who had emigrated earlier. The active recruitment of workers by the factory owners further multiplied the immigrant working force. The expansion of industries after 1867 and the creation of new employment opportunities, which attracted greater immigration, in turn led to the establishment of additional manufacturing and drew upon the expanding pool of labor. By 1880 there were dozens of firms besides Studebaker, Oliver, and Singer manufacturing agricultural machinery, wagons, furniture, boilers, oil stoves, pumps, barrels, brooms, stone pipe and cement, and wooden croquet sets.[4] Without the labor of immigrants, industrialization in South Bend would have developed at a much slower pace.

This emphasis upon the importance of the foreign-born as factory workers should not, however, be allowed to overshadow the role immigrants played as owners and inventors. John Chockelt, Frederick Colmer, and Henry Ginz were only a few of the entrepreneurs with immigrant backgrounds who contributed to the city's economic development. James Oliver's technological innovations and business success had a major impact on the general urban-industrial growth of South Bend, but there were others, like John Knoblock, who were important as owners and inventors.[5]

Nor was the leadership of immigrants restricted to specific businesses or industries. Throughout the thirty years after 1850 the names of immigrants and their children appear among the ranks of the community's social and political elite. The achievement of community leadership was closely related to how early in the city's development an individual came and how long he stayed. The immigrant who settled in South Bend before the Civil War, when the city was still small and its social and political institutions were in the initial stages of growth, had a better chance of achieving a position of leadership than those who came later. In the small-town atmosphere of the 1850s, newcomers quickly became known, and the process of adjustment and acceptance was carried out casually. Since everyone was essentially a newcomer, the foreign-born faced few disadvantages and no apparent prejudice. German and English immigrants found opportunities not only in business and skilled trades, but also in such important decision-making bodies as the city council or board of education.

As urban growth increased, however, new members of ethnic groups found assimilation more difficult and the achievement of community leadership more arduous, despite their proportionately greater numbers. Social divisions and residential restrictions were becoming more apparent by 1880 as the level of prejudice against new immigrants rose. In the more complex urban society that began to develop, the groups that were in a favorable position were those that possessed a well-formed set of social organizations. The voluntary association like the Germans' Turnverein served as both an agent of assimilation and a springboard to community leadership. In a society characterized by high rates of mobility, the ethnic organization was one of the key factors in the maintenance of cultural continuity and social stability. Since these organizations were often imitations of such native societies as the Masons or Odd Fellows, they served as an informal school for teaching native American values and ideals. Those individuals who learned their lessons well and possessed some talents for leadership could go on to enjoy a favorable reputation and position in the larger social community. Newer immigrant groups like the Poles, who arrived after the social framework of the city had begun to form and who failed to develop organizations that would promote assimilation, were delayed in their adjustment to the local society.

The story of South Bend's growth from village to city is one of people in motion. The role that the immigrant played in this story was a major one, for his restless movement, his search for a home and opportunity, was the bond that united him with thousands of other restless Americans in a single community. Although unlike both of them in many ways, South Bend and the hundreds of smaller cities like it were as important to the nation's growth as were the rural frontier and the spreading metropolis.

APPENDIX

Table A–1

BIRTHPLACE OF PERSONS, SOUTH BEND: 1870 and 1880
(By Ward)

Place of Birth	1870				1880					
	1	Ward 2,3[a]	4	Total	1	2	Ward 3	4	5	Total
Native-born (non-immigrant family)	864	3,164	735	4,763	1,260	2,113	1,054	1,147	1,540	7,114
Native-born (immigrant family)	261	597	356	1,214	519	507	855	640	426	2,947
Great Britain	13	40	20	73	27	37	13	30	35	142
Ireland	7	139	74	220	10	39	112	101	31	293
British America	7	47	87	141	36	52	23	111	25	247
Germany	166	258	95	519	199	164	79	162	106	710
Prussia	19	112	29	160	93	255	1,021	44	164	1,577
Other European	27	64	24	115	45	92	78	16	63	294
Total	1,364	4,421	1,420	7,205	2,189	3,259	3,235	2,251	2,390	13,324

Source: Manuscript federal census, 1870, 1880.

a. Census taker erroneously counted Second and Third wards together.

TABLE A–2

OCCUPATIONS OF IMMIGRANTS, SOUTH BEND: 1850–80
(In Percentages)

Occupation	British American				English				Irish			
	1850	1860	1870	1880	1850	1860	1870	1880	1850	1860	1870	1880
Professional	—	—	3%	4%	13%	5%	6%	3%	—	4%	7%	3%
Proprietors, managers, officials	—	2%	—	3	13	5	6	7	—	1	—	3
Semi-professional	—	—	—	—	—	—	2	3	—	—	—	—
Clerical sales	—	—	—	6	7	—	4	4	—	—	—	—
Petty proprietors, managers, officials	17%	17	4	1	27	16	6	3	33%	5	5	2
Skilled	50	27	44	34	27	53	28	28	—	12	23	34
Semiskilled and service	—	17	19	37	—	11	30	44	—	26	11	34
Unskilled and menial service	33	37	30	16	13	11	17	8	67	53	54	23

Table A-2—Continued

Occupation	German				Polish				Other Europeans				Native-Born of Foreign Parents			
	1850	1860	1870	1880	1850	1860	1870	1880	1850	1860	1870	1880	1850	1860	1870	1880
Professional	3%	1%	—	1%	—	—	1%	1%	13%	—	2%	2%	13%	2%	4%	2%
Proprietors, managers, officials	—	6	9%	6	—	—	1	1	—	3%	3	1	13	10	9	4
Semi-professional	—	1	—	1	—	—	1	—	—	—	—	—	—	—	—	1
Clerical sales	3	5	2	3	—	12%	1	1	—	10	5	—	7	7	9	12
Petty proprietors, managers, officials	23	7	8	9	—	12	7	2	50	13	—	5	20	12	2	3
Skilled	19	31	39	31	—	38	31	10	37	39	46	23	33	44	33	25
Semiskilled and service	23	30	26	34	—	25	12	77	—	19	21	58	7	—	26	37
Unskilled and menial service	29	20	16	16	—	13	45	8	—	16	23	11	7	24	16	16

Source: Manuscript federal census, 1850, 1860, 1870, 1880.

Table A–3
PROPERTY DISTRIBUTION FOR IMMIGRANTS, SOUTH BEND: 1850–70

Value of Property	Number of Persons Owning Property					
	1850		1860		1870	
	Real Estate	Personal	Real Estate	Personal	Real Estate	Personal
$ 0– 99	—	Not available	2	65	—	—
100– 199	2		10	63	1	71
200– 299	1		20	16	4	18
300– 399	—		22	9	4	12
400– 499	—		7	6	5	5
500– 599	7		19	5	11	20
600– 699	—		11	1	6	3
700– 799	—		1	—	2	1
800– 899	4		5	2	19	7
900– 999	1		1	—	—	—
1,000–1,499	4		29	7	50	11
1,500–1,999	—		5	2	42	5
2,000–2,499	3		7	3	20	13
2,500–4,999	1		12	1	43	17
5,000–7,499	—		2	1	24	11
7,500–9,999	—		—	1	4	1
10,000–over	—		—	—	23	9

Source: Manuscript federal census, 1850, 1860, 1870.

NOTES

PREFACE

1.   See Peter R. Knights, "A Method for Estimating Census Under-Enumeration," *Historical Methods Newsletter* 3 (Dec., 1969):5–8, and "Accuracy of Age Reporting in the Manuscript Federal Censuses of 1850 and 1860," *Historical Methods Newsletter* 4 (June, 1971):79–83; Sam B. Warner, Jr., *Streetcar Suburbs: The Process of Growth in Boston, 1870–1890* (Cambridge: Harvard University Press and MIT Press, 1962), pp. 171–78; and Harvey J. Graff, "Notes on Methods for Studying Literacy from the Manuscript Census," *Historical Methods Newsletter* 5 (Dec., 1971):11–16.

2.   T. G. Turner, ed., *Turner's South Bend Annual and Business Mirror* (South Bend: T. G. Turner, Publisher, 1871), p. 8.

3.   "The Historian and the Computer: A Simple Introduction to Complex Computation," *Essex Institute Historical Collections* 104 (Apr., 1968), 118.

CHAPTER 1

1.   Rowland Berthoff, *British Immigrants in Industrial America* (Cambridge: Harvard University Press, 1953): and Carl Wittke, *We Who Built America,* rev. ed. (Cleveland: Press of Case Western Reserve University, 1967). Charles N. Glaab and others have been cautious in classifying studies of urban immigrants as urban history because of the tendency to treat the city as only the setting. See Glaab, "The Historian and the American

City: A Bibliographic Survey," in *The Study of Urbanization,* ed. Philip M. Hauser and Leo F. Schnore (New York: John Wiley and Sons, 1965), p. 69.

2.   Among the best-known of the urban biographies are Bessie Pierce's *A History of Chicago,* 3 vols. (New York: Alfred A. Knopf, 1937–57); Constance McLaughlin Green's *Washington, Village and Capital, 1800–1878* (Princeton: Princeton University Press, 1962); and Bayrd Still's *Milwaukee, the History of a City* (Madison: State Historical Society of Wisconsin, 1948). Studies that deal with the role cities have played in important events or crucial periods are represented by Richard Wade, *Slavery in the Cities* (New York: Oxford University Press, 1964); Carl Bridenbaugh, *Cities in Revolt: Urban Life in America, 1743–1776* (New York: Alfred A. Knopf, 1955); or by William Miller, *Memphis during the Progressive Era: 1900–1917* (Memphis: Memphis State University Press, 1957).

3.   For example: Sam B. Warner, Jr., *Streetcar Suburbs: The Process of Urban Growth in Boston, 1870–1890* (Cambridge: Harvard University Press and MIT Press, 1962); George Dunlap, *The City in the American Novel, 1780–1900* (1934; reprinted, New York: Russell and Russell, 1965); or Morton and Lucia White, *The Intellectual versus the City* (Cambridge: Harvard University Press, 1962). There are a number of bibliographical articles which have attempted to place the major works in urban history into specific categories and which speculate on the merits of each interpretation. Among the most informative are those by Glaab, "Historian and the American City"; Roy Lubove, "The Urbanization Process: An Approach to Historical Research," *Journal of the American Institute of Planners* 33 (1967):33–39; and Dwight W. Hoover, "The Diverging Paths of American Urban History," *American Quarterly* 20 (1968):296–317.

4.   The most significant are: Stephan Thernstrom, "Reflections on the New Urban History," *Daedalus* 100 (1971):359–75; Eric Lampard, "American Historians and the Study of Urbanization, *American Historical Review* 67 (1961): 49–61; and "Urbanization and Social Change: On Broadening the Scope and Relevance of Urban History," in *The Historian and the City,* ed. Oscar Handlin and John Burchard (Cambridge: MIT Press, 1963). See also W. Stull Holt, "Some Consequences of the Urban Movement," *Pacific Historical Review* 22 (1953):337–52; R. Richard Wohl, "Urbanism, Urbanity, and the Historian," *University of Kansas City Review* 22 (1955):53–61.

5.   Hoover, "Diverging Paths," p. 305.

6.   Rowland Berthoff is one of several historians who have used mobility as the central theme in studying social history.

See *An Unsettled People: Social Order and Disorder in American History* (New York: Harper & Row, Publishers, 1971).

7.   Stephan Thernstrom, *Poverty and Progress: Social Mobility in a Nineteenth Century City* (Cambridge: Harvard University Press, 1964).

8.   Stephan Thernstrom and Richard Sennett, eds., *Nineteenth-Century Cities: Essays in the New Urban History* (New Haven: Yale University Press, 1969); Thernstrom and Peter R. Knights, "Men in Motion: Some Data and Speculations about Urban Population Mobility in Nineteenth-Century America," *Journal of Interdisciplinary History* 1 (1970):7–35; and Stephan Thernstrom, *The Other Bostonians: Poverty and Progress in the American Metropolis, 1800-1790* (Cambridge: Harvard University Press, 1973).

9.   *The Plain People of Boston, 1830–1860: A Study in City Growth* (New York: Oxford University Press, 1971).

10.   Howard P. Chudacoff, *Mobile Americans: Residential and Social Mobility in Omaha, 1880–1920* (New York: Oxford University Press, 1972).

11.   In addition to the several articles in Thernstrom and Sennett, *Nineteenth-Century Cities,* see Clyde Griffen, "Making It in America: Social Mobility in Mid-Nineteenth Century Poughkeepsie," *New York History* 51 (1970):479–99; Alwyn Barr, "Occupational and Geographic Mobility in San Antonio, 1870–1900," *Social Science Quarterly* 51 (1970):396–403; Richard J. Hopkins, "Occupational and Geographic Mobility in Atlanta, 1870–1896," *Journal of Southern History* 34 (1968): 200–13; William G. Robbins, "Opportunity and Persistence in the Pacific Northwest: A Quantitative Study of Early Roseburg, Oregon," *Pacific Historical Review* 39 (1970):279–96; Jay C. Dolan, "Immigrants in the City: New York Irish and German Catholics," *Church History* 41 (1972):354–68; and Paul B. Worthman, "Working Class Mobility in Birmingham, Alabama, 1880–1914," in *Anonymous Americans: Explorations in Nineteenth-Century Social History,* ed. Tamara K. Hareven (Englewood Cliffs, N.J.: Prentice-Hall, 1971), pp. 172–213.

12.   New York: Macmillan Co.

13.   New York: Oxford University Press, 1971.

14.   W. Lloyd Warner and Leo Srole, *Social Systems of American Ethnic Groups* (New Haven: Yale University Press, 1945). The authors followed a framework much like that originally constructed by Robert E. Park, which explains the effects the city has had on immigrants moving from a peasant or rural background to an urban culture. See Robert E. Park and Herbert A. Miller, *Old World Traits Transplanted* (New York: Harper

and Brothers, Publishers, 1921). Other sociological studies are Stanley Lieberson's *Ethnic Patterns in American Cities* (New York: Free Press of Glencoe, 1963); and Elin Anderson, *We Americans: A Study of Cleavage in an American City* (Cambridge: Harvard University Press, 1937).

15. Warner and Srole, *Social Systems,* p. 2.

16. Rev. ed. (Cambridge: University Press, 1959).

17. Ibid., pp. 57–61.

18. Ibid., pp. 216–17.

19. Ibid., p. 82.

20. New York: King's Crown Press, 1949.

21. *Immigrant City: Lawrence, Massachusetts, 1845–1921* (Chapel Hill: University of North Carolina Press, 1963), p. 42.

22. Ibid., pp. 67, 138–39. See also Moses Rischin, *The Promised City: New York's Jews, 1870–1914* (New York: Corinth Books, 1964); and Ralph Weld, *Brooklyn Is America* (New York: Columbia University Press, 1950).

23. Chudacoff, *Mobile Americans,* pp. 65, 70–71; and Humbert S. Nelli, *The Italians in Chicago, 1880–1930: A Study in Ethnic Mobility* (New York: Oxford University Press, 1970), p. 51.

24. U.S. Census Office, *Tenth Census of the United States* (1880), vol. 19, *Social Statistics of Cities* (Washington: Government Printing Office, 1887), p. 470.

25. Figures for the foreign stock are based on the original census enumerator's reports. *Foreign stock* is defined by E. P. Hutchinson as the foreign-born and their children. E. P. Hutchinson, *Immigrants and Their Children, 1850–1950* (New York: John Wiley and Sons, 1956), p. 3.

26. "The Urbanization of Human Population," in *Cities,* ed. *Scientific American* (New York: Alfred A. Knopf, 1966), p. 5.

27. Cf. Still, *Milwaukee,* pp. 230–53.

28. T. E. Howard, *A History of St. Joseph County, Indiana,* 2 vols. (Chicago: Lewis Publishing Co., 1907), 1:240. See also Agnes B. Hindelang, "The Social Development of South Bend, Indiana, as Shown by Its Ordinances" (master's thesis, University of Notre Dame, 1933), pp. 41, 61, 85. Douglas Laing Meikle, "James Oliver and the Oliver Chilled Plow Works" (dissertation, Indiana University, 1958), pp. 190, 204. See Bayrd Still, "Patterns of Mid-Nineteenth Century Urbanization in the Middle West," *Mississippi Valley Historical Review* 28 (1941):187–206.

29. Sam B. Warner, Jr., "If All the World Were Philadel-

phia: A Scaffolding for Urban History, 1774–1930," *American Historical Review* 74 (1968):41–42.

30.   Contemporaries were fully aware of the advantage which foreign-born laborers gave the city in attracting manufacturing. For example, see the comments supporting immigration in the *South Bend National Union,* February 29, 1868.

31.   Edwin Corle, *John Studebaker: An American Dream* (New York: E. P. Dutton and Co., 1948), p. 35; Albert Erskine, *History of the Studebaker Corporation* (South Bend: Studebaker Corporation, 1924), p. 15; Indiana Department of Statistics and Geology, *First Annual Report, 1879* (Indianapolis: Douglas and Carlon, 1879), p. 7; John Delaney, "The Beginnings of Industrial South Bend" (master's thesis, University of Notre Dame, 1951), p. 126.

32.   Thernstrom, *Poverty and Progress,* p. 196.

CHAPTER 2

1.   On Tuesday, Feb. 20, 1849, a group of 30 residents from South Bend, who had formed a joint-stock company, left for California. In the next few years several other similar companies were formed. In the spring of 1850 about 150 made the westward migration. See the *St. Joseph Valley Register,* Feb. 24, 1849, Jan. 3, 1850; *History of St. Joseph County, Indiana* (Chicago: Charles C. Chapman and Co., 1880), pp. 540–43.

2.   Unless otherwise noted, the information on individuals like Barth and on ethnic groups in South Bend is from the manuscript federal census returns for Portage Township and South Bend, 1850, 1860, 1870, 1880.

3.   There are several early histories of St. Joseph County that describe the origins of South Bend. The most informative and reliable is Timothy E. Howard, *A History of St. Joseph County, Indiana,* 2 vols. (Chicago: Lewis Publishing Co., 1907). See 1:130–32, 135, 138–39, 157–70, 173–76. A good account of South Bend's early commerce and competition for river trade is Otto M. Knoblock, *Early Navigation on the St. Joseph River, Publications of the Indiana Historical Society* 8 (Bloomington, 1925): 185–200.

4.   Leon Gordon, "The Influence of River Transportation on St. Joseph and Elkhart Counties, 1830–1860," *Indiana Magazine of History* 46 (1950):287.

5.   Mishawaka's decline or stagnation in the 1870s was partly caused by its lack of diversity and its dependence upon a single industry. After the failure of the iron deposits, the major in-

dustry was the wagon factory owned by George Milburn. After the 1872 fire, Milburn moved his company to Detroit, leaving Mishawaka with no other industry which could replace it. Indiana Department of Statistics and Geology, *Second Annual Report, 1880* (Indianapolis: Carlon and Hollenbeck, Printers and Binders, 1880), p. 258; *History of St. Joseph County,* pp. 790–92. South Bend built industrial power resources, too, to compete with Mishawaka: in 1844 the South Bend Manufacturing Co. completed a dam and two mill races. Anthony S. Kuharich, "Population Movements of South Bend, 1820–1930" (master's thesis, University of Notre Dame, 1941), p. 31.

6.   John D. Barnhart and Donald Carmony, *Indiana—From Frontier to Industrial Commonwealth,* 4 vols. (New York: Lewis Publishing Co., 1954), 2:11, 16, 294, 305, 307. During this same time the percentage of the total population for Indiana that was classified as urban more than doubled from 8.6 per cent to 19.5 per cent. South Bend's growth rate continued to be above average after 1880. At the close of the century it was the fifth-largest Indiana city, with 35,999 inhabitants. The *First Annual Report, 1879* of the Indiana Department of Statistics and Geology, p. 7, reported the population increase for each decade, the highest rate of growth being in the 1850s (44.11 per cent increase) and the lowest proportional growth in the 1880s (22.11 per cent).

7.   John J. Delaney, "The Beginnings of Industrial South Bend" (master's thesis, University of Notre Dame, 1951), pp. 110–11. The *St. Joseph Valley Register,* Dec. 13, 1866, commented briefly on the history of Lowell, which was founded in 1837. It was apparent that the residents hoped their "city" would some day become as great an industrial center as its namesake in Massachusetts. Probably the best short history of Lowell's brief existence is Edmund V. Campers, *History of St. Joseph's Parish, South Bend, Indiana, 1853–1953* (South Bend: privately printed, 1953), pp. 51–53. See also *Illustrated History of St. Joseph Church, South Bend, Indiana* (South Bend: 1901), unpaginated.

8.   Confusion for travelers sometimes resulted from this situation, since the street one block west of Michigan was actually named Main.

9.   T. G. Turner, ed., *Turner's South Bend Annual and Business Mirror, 1874* (South Bend: T. G. Turner, Publisher, 1874), p. 8; idem, *Directory of the Inhabitants, Institutions, and Manufactories of the City of South Bend, Indiana for 1880* (South Bend: Register Publishing Co., 1880), pp. 180, 196; *Holland's South Bend City Directory, 1867–8* (Chicago: Western Publishing Co., 1868), p. 113.

10.   Douglas Laing Meikle, "James Oliver and the Oliver

Chilled Plow Works" (dissertation, University of Indiana, 1958),
pp. 101, 111, 117.

11.　　See Turner, *Annual, 1876,* p. 3; Kuharich, "Population
Movements," p. 35; and Meikle, "James Oliver," pp. 144, 172,
225.

12.　　All of the daily newspapers carried the current crime
news and court activities. For example, see the *St. Joseph Valley
Register,* Oct. 16, 1873, and Jan. 1, 1874; or *South Bend Daily
Tribune,* Jan. 2 and 4, 1880.

13.　　*South Bend National Union,* Mar. 5, 1870; Agnes B.
Hindelang, "The Social Development of South Bend, Indiana,
as Shown by Its Ordinances" (master's thesis, University of
Notre Dame, 1933), p. 61; John B. Stoll, *An Account of St.
Joseph County from Its Origination* (Dayton: Dayton Historical
Publishing Co., 1923), p. 55; and Delaney, "Industrial South
Bend," p. 142.

14.　　Delaney, "Industrial South Bend," p. 143. After July,
1882, the power for lighting was supplied to the city by the South
Bend Electric Co. See Hindelang, "Social Development," p. 45.

15.　　*St. Joseph Valley Register,* May 21, 1868.

16.　　Coquillard's factory at the corner of Michigan and Market
streets was destroyed on Jan. 6, 1855—a Saturday, when the
building was empty. Although he had no insurance, Coquillard
rewarded each fireman with a small payment in gold. In a sense,
this fire represented something of the end of an era; Alexis
Coquillard, founder of the city, fell and was fatally injured while
inspecting the ruins. Otto M. Knoblock, "When South Bend Was
Young," *South Bend News-Times,* Apr. 21, 1935.

17.　　*History of St. Joseph Church.*

18.　　For example, see *South Bend Daily Tribune,* Apr. 5, 1880.
Chapman's *History of St. Joseph County,* p. 401, concludes that
the most frequent diseases were pneumonia, rheumatism, dysen-
tery, and diarrhea.

19.　　*South Bend Daily Tribune,* May 8, 1880. In the census
enumerator's report for 1880 all of the children of the Archambeau family, five boys and three girls, were reported as having
smallpox.

20.　　Ibid., June 8 and 24, July 1 and Aug. 1, 1880. See also
Hindelang, "Social Development," p. 56, for comments on the
conditions in the Third Ward.

21.　　Turner, *Directory, 1875,* p. 174, and *Directory, 1880,*
p. 199. See also Turner, *Annual, 1876,* p. 6.

22.　　*History of St. Joseph County,* p. 460; and Meikle, "James

Oliver," p. 190. See also Turner, *Directory, 1880,* p. 18; and Hindelang, "Social Development," pp. 34, 90, 92.

23.   *History of St. Joseph County,* p. 456.

24.   Delaney, "Industrial South Bend," pp. 108–9, 119–20; and Kuharich, "Population Movements," pp. 39–40.

25.   For comments on taxi service and traffic conditions, see the *South Bend Daily Tribune,* July 4, 1873, May 3, 1880, and July 1, 1880; and *St. Joseph Valley Register,* Mar. 8, 1878. Meikle, "James Oliver," p. 204, notes that the first bicycles were owned by Oliver's employees; but how extensively they were used as a method of getting to work is impossible to determine.

26.   See Howard, *St. Joseph County,* 12:240; *South Bend Daily Tribune,* Oct. 12, 1885; and Hindelang, "Social Development," pp. 83–86.

27.   Stoll, *Account of St. Joseph County,* p. 126; Kuharich, "Population Movements," p. 45; Indiana Department of Statistics and Geology, *First Annual Report, 1879,* p. 434; *National Union,* Jan. 1, 1870; and *South Bend Daily Tribune,* July 1, 1880.

28.   *National Union,* Jan. 1, 1870, and Feb. 5, 1870; *St. Joseph Valley Register,* Jan. 2, 1873; *South Bend Daily Tribune,* June 4, 1880, and Oct. 1, 1880; Stoll, *Account of St. Joseph County,* p. 131; and Howard, *St. Joseph County,* 1:216.

29.   *History of St. Joseph County,* pp. 581–85; Howard, *St. Joseph County,* 2:709; and *South Bend Daily Tribune,* May 3 and July 5, 1880.

30.   Kuharich, "Population Movements," p. 46; *St. Joseph Valley Register,* Apr. 22, 1861; Howard, *St. Joseph County,* 1:218; and *History of St. Joseph County,* p. 659.

31.   Barnhart and Carmony, *Indiana,* 1:342; Turner, *Directory, 1875,* p. 13; Stoll, *Account of St. Joseph County,* p. 110; Turner, *Annual, 1876,* p. 11; *St. Joseph Valley Register,* Jan. 13, 1870; and *News-Times,* June 16, 1935.

32.   *History of St. Joseph County,* p. 636. For information on the growing number of Catholic schools see *History of St. Joseph Church;* Turner, *Annual, 1870,* p. 11; Howard, *St. Joseph County,* 1:335; Campers, *St. Joseph's Parish,* p. 77; Kuharich, "Population Movements," pp. 48–49; Meikle, "James Oliver," pp. 87–88; and T. G. Turner, ed., *Gazetteer of St. Joseph Valley* (South Bend: T. G. Turner, Publisher, 1867).

33.   In addition to the free township and county libraries were at least two private libraries: McClure Working-Men's Library and the St. Joseph County Mercantile Library. *St. Joseph Valley Register,* Jan. 13, 1870.

34.   Ibid., Jan. 2, 1873; *South Bend Tribune,* July 4, 1873, and Mar. 9, 1932; *National Union,* Mar. 5, 1875; and Frederick Martin Chreist, "The History of the Professional Theater in South Bend, Indiana: 1855–1935" (master's thesis, Northwestern University, 1937), pp. 7–9, 17, 25, 43.

35.   *St. Joseph Valley Register,* Mar. 1, 1860; Turner, *Annual, 1869,* p. 2; *South Bend Daily Times,* Apr. 7, 1904; and Chreist, "Theater in South Bend," pp. 13, 33–34, 45.

CHAPTER 3

1.   For comments on Indiana's recruiting efforts see Frank Anthony Renkiewicz, "The Polish Settlement of St. Joseph County, Indiana: 1855–1935" (dissertation, University of Notre Dame, 1967), p. 32. A summary of population patterns in Indiana can be found in Conrad and Irene Taeuber, *The Changing Population of the United States* (New York: John Wiley and Sons, 1958), p. 62. For the statistics concerning Castle Garden see Robert Ernst, *Immigrant Life in New York City, 1825–1863* (New York: King's Crown Press, 1949), p. 189.

2.   The letter is in the collection of the Northern Indiana Historical Society, South Bend.

3.   *South Bend Daily Tribune,* Mar. 9, 1923; *St. Joseph Valley Register,* Mar. 17, 1880.

4.   Otto M. Knoblock, "When South Bend Was Young," *South Bend News-Times,* June 23, 1935.

5.   A German visitor to the city in 1864, Samuel Ludvigh, observed that a number of Bavarians came from Wunsiedel. *News-Times,* Apr. 7, 1904.

6.   Carl Wittke, *We Who Built America,* rev. ed. (Cleveland: Press of Case Western Reserve University, 1967), p. 424.

7.   The best study of Polish immigration is Renkiewicz, "Polish Settlement." See pp. 4, 30. See also Thomas T. McAvoy, *The History of the Catholic Church in the South Bend Area* (South Bend: Acquinas Library and Book Shop, 1953), unpaginated; and Anthony S. Kuharich, "Population Movements of South Bend, 1820–1930" (master's thesis, University of Notre Dame, 1941), p. 77.

8.   Renkiewicz believes many of the Poles came from the same districts in the old country. In 1885 there was a dispute whether the Poles had been actively recruited or had come of their own accord. The Immigration Commission of 1911, however, which questioned the officials of Studebaker and Oliver,

concluded that the immigrants had been encouraged to migrate.
See Renkiewicz, "Polish Settlement," pp. 33–34.

9.   The predominance of Germans and Irish among the foreign-born population was common not only in the state, but also
in other cities in Indiana—even in those, like Indianapolis, where
the number of ethnic residents was declining. See Frederick
Kershner, "From Country Town to Industrial City: The Urban
Pattern in Indianapolis," *Indiana Magazine of History* 45 (1949):
330. For comments on regional migration see David Ward,
*Cities and Immigrants: A Geography of Change in Nineteenth-
Century America* (New York: Oxford University Press, 1971),
pp. 66–67.

10.   The case of the French presented something of a problem in the use of the manuscript census reports. When the
information was coded, there was no special category for Alsace-
Lorraine, and immigrants born there were classified as French.
Some, however, who listed their birthplace as Alsace, were probably German-speaking immigrants. In the end, fortunately, there
was little distortion created by this ambiguity because only a few
immigrants from Alsace-Lorraine came to South Bend.

11.   For further comments on Swedish immigration, see Doug-
las Laing Meikle, "James Oliver and the Oliver Chilled Plow
Works" (dissertation, University of Indiana, 1958), p. 217; and
Kuharich, "Population Movements," pp. 98–99.

12.   Both families—"very respectable looking Belgians"—first
arrived in Mishawaka on Saturday, July 28, 1860. Some later
returned to Belgium, and others moved to South Bend. *Mishawaka Enterprise,* Aug. 4, 1860.

13.   *St. Joseph Valley Register,* Mar. 17, 1880; Meikle, "James
Oliver," p. 216; and *Mishawaka Enterprise,* Aug. 4, 1860.

14.   Otto M. Knoblock, "When South Bend Was Young,"
News-Times, June 23, 1935 and Mar. 1, 1910.

15.   Cf. Howard P. Chudacoff, *Mobile Americans: Residential
and Social Mobility in Omaha, 1880–1920* (New York: Oxford
University Press, 1972), p. 63.

16.   *Growth of Cities in the Nineteenth Century: A Study in
Statistics* (New York: Macmillan Co., 1899), p. 259. See also
Peter R. Knights, *The Plain People of Boston, 1830–1860: A
Study in City Growth* (New York: Oxford University Press,
1971), pp. 33–47.

17.   Several other sources support the conclusion that these
were the states which sent the greatest number of immigrants to
Indiana. U.S. Census Office, *Tenth Census of the United States*
(1880), vol. 1, *Statistics of the Population* (Washington: Government Printing Office, 1883), pp. 475 and 506; Elfrieda Lang, "An

Analysis of Northern Indiana's Population in 1850," *Indiana Magazine of History* 49 (1953):18–19; John D. Barnhart and Donald F. Carmony, *Indiana—From Frontier to Industrial Commonwealth,* 4 vols. (New York: Lewis Publishing Co., 1954), 2:295; Wittke, *We Who Built America,* p. 197; and McAvoy, *Catholic Church in the South Bend Area.* See also Ward, *Cities and Immigrants,* p. 57.

18.   Kuharich, "Population Movements," p. 92.

19.   Merle Curti, *The Making of an American Community: A Case Study of Democracy in a Frontier Community* (Stanford: Stanford University Press, 1959), p. 68; and Mildred Throne, "A Population Study of an Iowa County in 1850," *Iowa Journal of History* 57 (1959):308–10.

20.   Blake McKelvey, *Rochester: The Flower City, 1855–1890* (Cambridge: Harvard University Press, 1949), p. 3 n.; Stuart M. Blumin, "Mobility in a Nineteenth-Century American City: Philadelphia, 1820–1860" (dissertation, University of Pennsylvania, 1968), p. 107; Chudacoff, *Mobile Americans,* p. 40; and Stephan Thernstrom and Peter R. Knights, "Men in Motion: Some Data and Speculations about Urban Population Mobility in Nineteenth-Century America," *Journal of Interdisciplinary History* 1 (1970):11–12.

21.   The annual out-migration rates can be determined by using the city directories. Since the South Bend directories, however, do not contain a report of the number of names expunged from the preceding year's directory (as do those of such other cities as Boston) and since the directories do not distinguish between foreign- and native-born, it was not practical to determine the gross population turnover. For an example of this laborious but generally unused method of determining annual out-migration rates, see Thernstrom and Knights, "Men in Motion," pp. 13–23.

22.   *Mishawaka Enterprise,* Apr. 23, 1859; *St. Joseph Valley Register,* Apr. 5 and 26, 1860.

CHAPTER 4

1.   David R. Leeper, *Early Inns and Taverns of South Bend, Indiana* (South Bend: Helen Hibberd Ware, Rare and Used Books, n.d.), pp. 17–18.

2.   Manuscript federal census, 1880; and Timothy E. Howard, *A History of St. Joseph County, Indiana,* 2 vols. (Chicago: Lewis Publishing Co., 1907), 1: 439.

3.   Donald B. Cole, *Immigrant City: Lawrence, Massachusetts,*

1845–1921 (Chapel Hill: University of North Carolina Press, 1963), p. 108. For a discussion of some of the problems involved in determining the relationship to the head of the household, see Lawrence A. Glasco, "Computerizing the Manuscript Census," *Historical Methods Newsletter* 3 (1969):1–4; and David Herlihy, "Computerizing the Manuscript Census—A Comment," *Historical Methods Newsletter* 4 (1970):9–13.

4.   Chapin's house was at 407 West Navarre Street. The Clem Studebaker house, built in 1886 in the "midwestern Romanesque" style, was another of the more impressive nineteenth-century homes. *Indiana Houses of the Nineteenth Century* (Indianapolis: Indiana Historical Society, 1962), p. 88.

5.   Oscar Handlin, *Boston's Immigrants: A Study in Acculturation,* rev. ed. (Cambridge: Harvard University Press, 1959), p. 329.

6.   Ibid. In New York the average number of persons per dwelling was 16.37. U.S. Census Office, *Tenth Census of the United States* (1880), vol. 1, *Statistics of the Population* (Washington: Government Printing Office, 1883), pp. 670–71.

7.   The following figures illustrate the housing density of the immigrants in South Bend:

Year	Number of Immigrant Dwellings	Average Number Persons per Dwelling
1850	61	4.33
1860	206	5.35
1870	353	6.39
1880	759	7.18

Source: Manuscript federal census, 1850, 1860, 1870, 1880.

8.   Robert E. Park, *Human Communities* (Glencoe, Ill.: The Free Press, 1952), p. 170. Donald Cole (*Immigrant City,* p. 109) found this pattern to be true of Lawrence, Mass. Richard C. Wade agrees that the outer rings of nineteenth-century cities were occupied by "the older inhabitants, usually wealthier than others," but he qualifies his statement by pointing out that with improved transportation there was constant movement within the cities, even among the ethnic neighborhoods. Hence the stable ethnic ghetto never really existed. "Urbanization," in *The Comparative Approach to American History,* ed. C. Vann Woodward (New York: Basic Books, 1968), pp. 193–94. See also Otis D. and Beverly Duncan, "Residential Distribution and Occupational Stratification," *American Journal of Sociology* 60 (1955):500–501; and David Ward, *Cities and Immigrants: A Geography of*

Change in Nineteenth-Century America (New York: Oxford University, Press, 1971), pp. 105–9.

9. Sam Bass Warner, Jr., "If All the World Were Philadelphia: A Scaffolding for Urban History, 1774–1930," *American Historical Review* 74 (1968):33–35; and *The Private City: Philadelphia in Three Periods of Its Growth* (Philadelphia: University of Pennsylvania Press, 1968), pp. 56–57. Stuart Blumin, "Mobility and Change in Ante-Bellum Philadelphia," in *Nineteenth-Century Cities: Essays in the New Urban History,* ed. Stephan Thernstrom and Richard Sennett (New Haven: Yale University Press, 1969), p. 188; Humbert S. Nelli, *Italians in Chicago, 1880–1930: A Study in Ethnic Mobility* (New York: Oxford University Press, 1970), p. 45; and Howard P. Chudacoff, *Mobile Americans: Residential and Social Mobility in Omaha, 1880–1920* (New York: Oxford University Press, 1972), pp. 65–67. See also Ward, *Cities and Immigrants,* pp. 105–7.

10. Karl E. and Alma F. Taeuber in *Negroes in Cities: Residential Segregation and Neighborhood Change* (Chicago: Aldine Publishing Co., 1965), pp. 243–44, suggest that the Gini concentration index and the index of dissimilarity are both well suited for determining the degree of segregation. For a technical explanation and evaluation of several indexes of residential segregation, see pp. 195–245.

11. Only 1870 and 1880 could be used here; the 1850 and 1860 censuses did not record wards.

12. Oliver usually imported Belgian workers in groups. For example, on Mar. 13, 1880, seventeen arrived and went to work in his plow factory. *St. Joseph Valley Register,* Mar. 17, 1880.

13. Cf. Leo F. Schnore and Peter R. Knights, "Residence and Social Structure: Boston in the Ante-Bellum Period," in *Nineteenth-Century Cities,* ed. Thernstrom and Sennett, p. 254.

14. Robert Ernst, *Immigrant Life in New York City, 1825–1863* (New York: King's Crown Press, 1949), pp. 43–44. Rowland Berthoff has observed that the British maintained higher economic standards, which enabled them to live outside the "foreign" districts. Their distaste for living with other language groups presumably made them similar in sentiment to the native Americans. See Berthoff, *British Immigrants in Industrial America, 1790–1950* (Cambridge: Harvard University Press, 1953), p. 134.

15. Edmund V. Campers, *History of St. Joseph's Parish, South Bend, Indiana, 1853–1953* (South Bend: privately printed, 1953), p. 44.

16. Manuscript federal census, 1870. During most years French immigrants continued to be scattered throughout the city, many of them working as factory operatives.

17.   The federal enumerator's lists and city directories for the Fourth Ward in 1870 and 1880, systematically studied, corroborate the parish censuses found in Campers, *St. Joseph's Parish,* pp. 56–58. See also C. N. Fassett, "Scenes of Early Activities in the Lives of People Who Helped Build South Bend," *South Bend Tribune,* July 29, 1916.

18.   *A Guide to the University of Notre Dame and the Academy of St. Mary of the Immaculate Conception, near South Bend, Indiana* (Philadelphia: J. B. Chandler, Printer, 1865), p. 10.

19.   Cf. Handlin, *Boston's Immigrants,* pp. 96, 98.

20.   *South Bend Weekly Tribune,* July 4, 1873.

21.   Thomas T. McAvoy, *The History of the Catholic Church in the South Bend Area* (South Bend: Acquinas Library and Book Shop, 1953), unpaginated. See also Frank Anthony Renkiewicz, "The Polish Settlement of St. Joseph County, Indiana: 1855–1935" (dissertation, University of Notre Dame, 1967), pp. 36, 42.

22.   Cf. the indexes of dissimilarity for Omaha in Chudacoff, *Mobile Americans,* p. 66.

23.   Fassett, "Scenes of Early Activities."

24.   See Stephan Thernstrom, *Poverty and Progress: Social Mobility in a Nineteenth-Century City* (Cambridge: Harvard University Press, 1964), pp. 90–96. Peter R. Knights, *The Plain People of Boston, 1830–1860: A Study in City Growth* (New York: Oxford University Press, 1971), pp. 149–56, has published his classification system, which is also based on Thernstrom's model and is similar to the one used for South Bend. The organization of occupations according to the nature of the work involved was also used by both Merle Curti and Oscar Handlin in their pioneer studies of population in the nineteenth century. See Curti, *The Making of an American Community: A Case Study of Democracy in a Frontier Community* (Stanford: Stanford University Press, 1959), pp. 58–61; and Handlin, *Boston's Immigrants,* pp. 235, 251–52. Two essays that explore some of the difficulties of using occupational information are Clyde Griffen, "Occupational Mobility in Nineteenth-Century America: Problems and Possibilities," *Journal of Social History* 5 (1972):310–30; and Michael B. Katz, "Occupational Classification in History," *Journal of Interdisciplinary History* 3 (1972):63–88.

25.   See Thernstrom, *Poverty and Progress,* pp. 15–32, for an excellent summary of the conditions of the laborer in the mid-nineteenth century.

26.   Indiana Department of Statistics and Geology, *First An-*

nual Report, 1879 (Indianapolis: Douglas and Carlon, 1879), p. 395.

27.   Knights, *Plain People,* p. 75, found immigrant mobility within Boston's core and even between core and periphery at times of high mobility. South Bend, however, before 1880 was not large enough to consider in terms of core and periphery.

28.   *Holland's South Bend City Directory* (Chicago: Western Publishing Co., 1867–68), p. 129; and T. G. Turner, ed., *Directory of the Inhabitants, Institutions, and Manufactories of the City of South Bend, Indiana* (South Bend: T. G. Turner, Publisher, 1875), pp. 167–68.

29.   Turner, *Directory, 1875,* pp. 92, 97.

30.   Ibid., p. 168; and the manuscript federal census, 1880.

31.   Chudacoff, *Mobile Americans,* p. 108, found that in Omaha the large majority of workers were not influenced in their choice of residence by where they worked. Chudacoff, however, studied Omaha in the period 1880–1920, when mass transit was available to workers. In South Bend mass transit facilities were inadequate before 1880.

CHAPTER 5

1.   *South Bend Daily Tribune,* July 5, 1880; Douglas Laing Meikle, "James Oliver and the Oliver Chilled Plow Works" (dissertation, University of Indiana, 1958), pp. 206, 217–18; and Otto M. Knoblock, "When South Bend Was Young," *South Bend News-Times,* June 9, 1935.

2.   See Anderson and Cooley, *South Bend and the Men Who Have Made It* (South Bend: Tribune Printing Co., 1901), p. 99; Knoblock, "When South Bend Was Young," *News-Times,* June 9, 1935; and Meikle, "James Oliver," pp. 45, 98, 164.

3.   *South Bend Daily Tribune,* Mar. 9, 1922; *History of St. Joseph County, Indiana* (Chicago: Charles C. Chapman and Co., 1880), p. 27. See also Anderson and Cooley, *South Bend,* pp. 110–11; and *St. Joseph Valley Register,* May 8, 1873. In March 1875 Knoblock and his partners purchased the Indiana Reaper and Iron Co. for twenty thousand dollars and renamed it the St. Joseph Reaper and Machine Co. On Aug. 8, 1878, this company was reorganized into the South Bend Chilled Plow Co. Meikle, "James Oliver," pp. 173, 188, 191. *St. Joseph Valley Register,* Aug. 8, 1878.

4.   Stephan Thernstrom, *Poverty and Progress: Social Mobility in a Nineteenth Century City* (Cambridge: Harvard University Press, 1964), p. 83; italics in original.

5.   In a sociological examination of social mobility, Eli Chinoy has stated that "there seems ample warrant for concluding that in American society, at least, occupation is probably the most significant, that is it is more likely to influence other variables than to be influenced by them." "Social Mobility Trends in the United States," *American Sociological Review* 20 (1955):180–86. See also Oscar Handlin, "The Social System," *Daedalus* 90 (1961):13. Chinoy's view has been countered by warnings against over-dependence on occupation to determine class status; see Eric E. Lampard in Peter R. Knights, *The Plain People of Boston, 1830–1860: A Study in City Growth* (New York: Oxford University Press, 1971), p. 194.

6.   Seldom did the want ads in the press offer anything but housework in private homes. A few factory positions were available, some of them at the Eagle Knitting Co. of Elkhart, which advertised for twenty-five girls to run its machines. See for example *South Bend Daily Tribune,* Sept. 21, 1877, or June 8, 1880.

7.   Indiana Department of Statistics and Geology, *First Annual Report, 1879* (Indianapolis: Douglas and Carlon, 1879), p. 163.

8.   An early glassblowing enterprise failed, as did the woolen mill that Captain Anthony Defrees opened in 1831. Anthony S. Kuharich, "Population Movements of South Bend, 1820–1930" (master's thesis, University of Notre Dame, 1941), p. 30. For early industrial development see John J. Delaney, "The Beginnings of Industrial South Bend" (master's thesis, University of Notre Dame, 1951), pp. 8–9, 14–16; *The City of South Bend, Indiana* (South Bend: South Bend Hydraulic Co., 1866), p. 5. For flour production in later years see T. G. Turner, ed., *Turner's South Bend Annual and Business Mirror, 1871* (South Bend: T. G. Turner, Publisher, 1871), p. 6, *1874,* p. 8, *1876,* p. 7; Turner's *Directory of the Inhabitants, Institutions, and Manufactories of the City of South Bend, Indiana* (South Bend: T. G. Turner, Publisher, 1875), p. 18; and Indiana Department of Statistics and Geology, *First Annual Report, 1879,* p. 225.

9.   Donald Carmony, "Cars from an Anvil: The Studebaker Saga," *American Heritage,* n.s. 2 (1950–51):3; Delaney, "Industrial South Bend," pp. 96, 122. Alexis Coquillard and George Milburn both opened wagon factories before 1869. Kuharich, "Population Movements," p. 35; and Delaney, "Industrial South Bend," pp. 100, 125.

10.   Allan Nevins, *The Emergence of Modern America, 1865–1878,* vol. 8 in Arthur M. Schlesinger and Dixon Ryan Fox, eds., *A History of American Life* (New York: Macmillan Co., 1927), pp. 45–46.

11.   Kuharich, "Population Movements," p. 31; Meikle, "James Oliver," p. 98; Delaney, "Industrial South Bend," p. 125; and Edwin Corle, *John Studebaker: An American Dream* (New York: E. P. Dutton and Co., 1948), p. 146.

12.   See *St. Joseph Valley Register,* Mar. 17, 1880; Meikle, "James Oliver," pp. 216–17; Frank Anthony Renkiewicz, "The Polish Settlement of St. Joseph County, Indiana: 1855–1935" (dissertation, University of Notre Dame, 1967), p. 33; and Turner, *Directory, 1880,* pp. 177–78, 203.

13.   See Natalie Rogoff, "Recent Trends in Urban Occupational Mobility," in *Class, Status and Power,* ed. Seymour M. Lipset and Reinhard Bendix, 2nd ed. (New York: Free Press of Glencoe, 1966), p. 144; and Seymour M. Lipset and Reinhard Bendix, *Social Mobility in Industrial Society* (Berkeley: University of California Press, 1959), p. 204.

14.   A brief summary of Thernstrom's attack on the blocked mobility hypothesis, which was a part of his larger study on Newburyport, is contained in "Notes on the Historical Study of Social Mobility," in *Quantitative History,* ed. Don Karl Rowney and James Q. Graham, Jr. (Homewood, Ill.: Dorsey Press, 1969), pp. 102–5. See also Oscar Handlin, "The Social System," *Daedalus* 90 (1961):13.

15.   See Indiana Department of Statistics and Geology, *First Annual Report, 1879,* pp. 391–95. Cf. U.S. Census Office, *Tenth Census of the United States* (1880), vol. 20, *Statistics of Wages in Manufacturing Industries* (Washington: Government Printing Office, 1886), p. 414.

16.   The *St. Joseph Valley Register,* Jan. 2, 1873, reported that a number of carpenters and joiners worked for Studebaker.

17.   Humbert S. Nelli, *Italians in Chicago, 1880–1930: A Study in Ethnic Mobility* (New York: Oxford University Press, 1970), pp. 49–51; Clyde Griffen, "Workers Divided: The Effect of Craft and Ethnic Differences in Poughkeepsie, New York, 1850–1880," in *Nineteenth-Century Cities: Essays in the New Urban History,* ed. Stephan Thernstrom and Richard Sennett (New Haven: Yale University Press, 1969), p. 62. Howard P. Chudacoff, *Mobile Americans: Residential and Social Mobility in Omaha, 1880– 1920* (New York: Oxford University Press, 1972), pp. 86–87, found that occupational status had less effect on the mobility rates of the foreign-born than on those of the native Americans.

18.   Thernstrom, *Poverty and Progress,* pp. 200–205.

19.   Ibid., pp. 205–6.

20.   Bayrd Still, *Milwaukee, The History of a City* (Madison: State Historical Society of Wisconsin, 1948), p. 112.

21.   Robert Ernst, *Immigrant Life in New York City, 1825–1863* (New York: King's Crown Press, 1949), pp. 79–81, 87; and Griffen, "Workers Divided," p. 76.

22.   Turner, *Directory, 1880,* p. 184.

23.   Oscar Handlin, *The Uprooted* (Boston: Little, Brown and Co., 1951), p. 91.

24.   Rowland Berthoff, *British Immigrants in Industrial America, 1790–1950* (Cambridge: Harvard University Press, 1953), pp. 69, 122, 125, 129–30, 211.

25.   Ernst, *Immigrant Life,* p. 95.

26.   Oscar Handlin, *Boston's Immigrants: A Study in Acculturation,* rev. ed. (Cambridge: Harvard University Press, 1959), p. 216. Cf. Ernst, *Immigrant Life,* p. 69; Donald B. Cole, *Immigrant City: Lawrence, Massachusetts, 1845–1921* (Chapel Hill: University of North Carolina Press, 1963), p. 124; Thernstrom, *Poverty and Progress,* p. 27, and "Immigrants and Wasps: Ethnic Differences in Occupational Mobility in Boston, 1890–1940," in *Nineteenth-Century Cities,* p. 150; and Griffen, "Workers Divided, p. 81.

27.   Handlin, *Boston's Immigrants,* p. 59; and Kate H. Claghorn, "The Foreign Immigrant in New York City," U.S. Industrial Commission Report (Washington: Government Printing Office, 1901), 15: 462.

28.   Downward mobility rates of Omaha and South Bend were lower than those of eastern cities. Cf. Chudacoff, *Mobile Americans,* pp. 100–101.

29.   Turner, *Directory, 1880,* p. 18; *Illustrated Historical Atlas of St. Joseph County, Indiana* (Chicago: Higgins, Beldon and Co., 1875), p. 15.

30.   *St. Joseph Valley Register,* Jan. 13, 1870. These values of homes in South Bend are lower than those in Boston, where—as Sam B. Warner, Jr., estimates—middle-class suburban homes in the last third of the nineteenth century cost from two to four thousand dollars or more. *Streetcar Suburbs: The Process of Urban Growth in Boston, 1870–1890* (Cambridge: Harvard University Press and MIT Press, 1962), p. 127.

31.   Thernstrom, *Poverty and Progress,* p. 28.

32.   Ibid.; and Griffen, "Workers Divided," p. 70.

CHAPTER 6

1.   Oscar Handlin, "The Social System," *Daedalus* 90 (1961): 23. See also Merle Curti, *The Making of an American Commu-*

nity: A Case Study of Democracy in a Frontier Community
(Stanford: Stanford University Press, 1959), p. 417.

2.   The Canadian in this case, John Haggerty, was a descendant of Irish parents and therefore obviously not a French Canadian.

3.   Curti, *American Community,* pp. 418, 424.

4.   Ibid., p. 421. Mildred Thorne found that the largest percentage of community leaders in Wapello County, Iowa, in 1850 were between thirty-one and forty years of age. "A Population Study of an Iowa County in 1850," *Iowa Journal of History* 57 (1959):327.

5.   *Laws and Ordinances of the City of South Bend, Indiana* (South Bend: Times Publishing Co., 1905), p. 21.

6.   Douglas Laing Meikle, "James Oliver and the Oliver Chilled Plow Works" (dissertation, University of Indiana, 1958), p. 172.

7.   Anderson and Cooley, *South Bend and the Men Who Have Made It* (South Bend: Tribune Printing Co., 1901), p. 111.

8.   *History of St. Joseph County, Indiana* (Chicago: Charles C. Chapman and Co., 1880), p. 916.

9.   *St. Joseph Valley Register,* July 13, 1871.

10.   *History of St. Joseph County,* p. 916; and *South Bend Daily Tribune,* Feb. 7, 1880.

11.   Not to be confused with George Matthews, the stepfather of Schuyler Colfax.

12.   *History of St. Joseph County,* pp. 856–57, 558; *Laws and Ordinances,* p. 213.

13.   Frank Anthony Renkiewicz, "The Polish Settlement of St. Joseph County, Indiana: 1855–1935" (dissertation, University of Notre Dame, 1967), p. 60.

14.   Frederick Martin Chreist, "The History of the Professional Theater in South Bend, Indiana" (master's thesis, Northwestern University, 1937), p. 11; *South Bend Morning Herald,* May 9, 1876. Cf. Oscar Handlin, *The Uprooted* (Boston: Little, Brown and Co., 1951), p. 181, who states that "more even than the press, the stage was the vehicle of popular culture in the second half of the nineteenth century."

15.   *South Bend National Union,* Feb. 5, 1870.

16.   *South Bend Times,* Nov. 8, 1908; and *South Bend Daily Tribune,* July 29, 1878.

17.   *South Bend Weekly Tribune,* July 6, 1876; *South Bend*

Times, Sept. 18, 1910; and *South Bend Daily Tribune,* July 5, 1880.

18.   The Turnverein was organized in 1861, Germania Lodge No. 301 (Masons) in 1865, and the Robert Blum Lodge No. 278 (Odd Fellows) in 1867. *St. Joseph Valley Register,* Jan. 13, 1870.

19.   *South Bend Daily Tribune,* May 3, 1880, and *South Bend Times,* Nov. 8, 1908. Cf. Robert Ernst, *Immigrant Life in New York City, 1825–1863* (New York: King's Crown Press, 1949), p. 127; and Carl Wittke, *We Who Built America,* rev. ed. (Cleveland: Press of Case Western Reserve University, 1967), p. 212. T. G. Turner, ed., *Directory of the Inhabitants, Institutions, and Manufactories of the City of South Bend, Indiana for 1880* (South Bend: Register Printing Co., 1880), p. 99.

20.   *National Union,* Jan. 1, 1870; *South Bend Daily Tribune,* July 29, 1878; and *History of St. Joseph County,* pp. 925–26.

21.   See Handlin, *Uprooted,* pp. 185, 193; and idem, "Historical Perspectives on the American Ethnic Groups," *Daedalus* 90 (1961):230.

22.   Rowland Berthoff, *British Immigrants in Industrial America, 1790–1950* (Cambridge: Harvard University Press, 1953), pp. 165–84. The failure to organize separate societies was apparent in Lawrence, Mass., and Boston also. See Donald B. Cole, *Immigrant City: Lawrence, Massachusetts, 1845–1921* (Chapel Hill: University of North Carolina Press, 1963), p. 43; and Oscar Handlin, *Boston's Immigrants: A Study in Acculturation,* rev. ed. (Cambridge: Harvard University Press, 1959), p. 220.

23.   *St. Joseph Valley Register,* June 3, 1876; *South Bend Weekly Tribune,* Jan. 25, 1875; and Anthony S. Kuharich, "Population Movements of South Bend, 1820–1930" (master's thesis, University of Notre Dame, 1941), p. 145.

24.   Renkiewicz, "Polish Settlement," pp. 39, 42. The *South Bend Weekly Tribune,* Jan. 21, 1875, estimated that combined membership in the two Polish societies was equal to only about 5 or 10 per cent of the Polish population. The pattern of social organization in South Bend was similar to that found by Robert E. Park and Herbert A. Miller, *Old World Traits Transplanted* (New York: Harper and Brothers, Publishers, 1921), pp. 211–12.

25.   See for example the *South Bend Tribune,* Nov. 28, 1873; Nov. 29, 1873; *South Bend Weekly Tribune,* Nov. 3, 1875; June 24, 1876; and July 29, 1878.

26.   *St. Joseph County Forum,* Oct. 9, 1858; *South Bend Weekly Tribune,* Oct. 1, 1880; Apr. 19, 1875; and Oct. 23, 1875.

27.   *South Bend Tribune,* Nov. 29, 1873. See also Renkiewicz, "Polish Settlement," p. 38. Lewis Atherton, *Main Street on the*

Middle Border (Bloomington: Indiana University Press, 1966), pp. 103–4, has also noted that newspapers frequently treated social happenings in the poorer districts of midwestern towns with levity or criticism.

CHAPTER 7

1. Stephan Thernstrom, *Poverty and Progress: Social Mobility in a Nineteenth Century City* (Cambridge: Harvard University Press, 1964), p. 103.

2. Howard P. Chudacoff, *Mobile Americans: Residential and Social Mobility in Omaha, 1880–1920* (New York: Oxford University Press, 1972), pp. 69–71.

3. In some ways the residential patterns of South Bend's immigrants were similar to those in Poughkeepsie, N.Y., a small city which had also undergone a change from commerce to modest industrialization in the mid-nineteenth century. The principal difference is that in Poughkeepsie ethnic segregation was more distinct. Clyde Griffen, "Workers Divided: The Effect of Craft and Ethnic Differences in Poughkeepsie, New York, 1850–1880," in *Nineteenth-Century Cities: Essays in the New Urban History*, ed. Stephan Thernstrom and Richard Sennett (New Haven: Yale University Press, 1969), pp. 89, 91.

4. T. G. Turner, ed., *Directory of the Inhabitants, Institutions, and Manufactories of the City of South Bend, Indiana for 1880* (South Bend: Register Printing Co., 1880), pp. 177–203. For a good theoretical analysis of the relation between population growth and industrialization see Allan R. Pred, *The Spatial Dynamics of U.S. Urban-Industrial Growth, 1800–1914*, Regional Science Studies Series (Cambridge: MIT Press, 1966), pp. 38–41, 79. See also Adna F. Weber, *The Growth of Cities in the Nineteenth Century: A Study in Statistics* (New York: Macmillan Co., 1899), pp. 185–209.

5. Knoblock invented a "jointer" which improved plow production. Douglas Laing Meikle, "James Oliver and the Oliver Chilled Plow Works" (dissertation, University of Indiana, 1958), p. 188. Pred discusses the importance of inventions and innovations for urban-industrial expansion in *Spatial Dynamics*, pp. 25–28, 60, 88.

A NOTE ON SOURCES

Since many of the sources used in this study have already been cited or commented on in the chapter notes, I will not attempt to list a full bibliography here. There are of course a great number of books that are relevant to the study of urbanization and immigration. A more complete bibliography of sources used in this analysis of South Bend may be found in my dissertation, "The Urbanization of South Bend's Immigrants, 1850–1880" (University of Notre Dame, 1972).

The manuscript federal census provided the most abundant information about the individual immigrants. There are more and more articles on the use of these census records in journals such as *Historical Methods Newsletter, Journal of Interdisciplinary History,* and *Journal of Social History.* Some useful suggestions can be found in Robert G. Barrows, "The Manuscript Federal Census: Source for a 'New' Local History," *Indiana Magazine of History* 69 (1973): 181–92; George A. Boeck, "A Historical Note on the Uses of Census Returns," *Mid-America* 44 (1962): 46–50; or Margaret Walsh, "The Census as an Accurate Source of Information: The Value of Mid-Nineteenth Century Manufacturing Returns," *Historical Methods Newsletter* 3 (1970): 3–13. The regularly published results or compilations of the federal census are also valuable. Unfortunately Indiana, unlike such other states as Massachusetts, did not conduct a state census in the years between 1850 and 1880. The only supplements to the federal records are the parish censuses for South Bend's Fourth Ward reported in Edmund V. Campers, *History of St. Joseph's Parish, South Bend, Indiana, 1853–1953* (1953).

Important for locating the residences of immigrants who had
first been identified in the census was *Holland's South Bend City
Directory* (Chicago: Western Publishing Co.) for 1867 and
1868 and the city directories edited and published by T. G.
Turner between 1869 and 1880. Turner's *Gazetteer of St. Joseph
Valley* for 1867 and 1869, and *Turner's South Bend Annual and
Business Mirror* (1869–71, 1874, 1876), as well as *The City of
South Bend, Indiana* published by the South Bend Hydraulic Co.
(South Bend: 1866), are good sources for the economic and industrial growth of South Bend. Leon M. Gordon's "The Influence
of River Transportation on St. Joseph and Elkhart Counties,
1830–1860," *Indiana Magazine of History* 46 (1950): 283–96,
and Otto M. Knoblock's *Early Navigation on the St. Joseph
River,* Publications of the Indiana Historical Society, 8 (Bloomington, 1925) both provide brief sketches of the early economic
life of South Bend and the surrounding region. Other basic information valuable to understanding and measuring South Bend's
urban growth is found in *Laws and Ordinances of the City of
South Bend, Indiana* (South Bend: Times Publishing Co., 1905)
and Elfrieda Lang, "An Analysis of Northern Indiana's Population in 1850," *Indiana Magazine of History* 49 (1953):17–60.
David R. Leeper's *Early Inns and Taverns of South Bend, Indiana*
(South Bend: Helen Hibberd Ware, Rare and Used Books, n.d.)
proved to be of only limited use.

There are a number of atlases and maps that describe South
Bend's physical expansion and readjustments. The two most
valuable were the *Illustrated Historical Atlas of St. Joseph
County, Indiana* (Chicago: Higgins, Belden and Co., 1875) and
the *Illustrated Historical Atlas of the State of Indiana* (Chicago:
Baskin, Förster, 1876). Several local and county histories contain an abundance of detailed information about specific individuals, political offices and elections, social organizations, religion,
education, and business or industrial growth. The biographies in
Chapman's *History of St. Joseph County, Indiana* (Chicago:
Charles C. Chapman and Co., 1880) are good, but Timothy E.
Howard's *A History of St. Joseph County, Indiana,* 2 vols. (Chi-
cago: Lewis Publishing Co., 1907) offers the most information
on South Bend. Other local histories of more limited value are
Anderson and Cooley, *South Bend and the Men Who Have Made
It* (South Bend: Tribune Printing Co., 1901), John B. Stoll,
An Account of St. Joseph County from Its Origination (Dayton:
Dayton Historical Publishing Co., 1923), and Thomas T. Mc-
Avoy, *The History of the Catholic Church in the South Bend
Area* (South Bend: Acquinas Library and Bookshop, 1953).
There is still a need for a good history of South Bend's major
industries. Albert Erskine's *History of the Studebaker Corpora-
tion* (South Bend: Studebaker Corporation, 1924), and Edwin
Corle's *John Studebaker: An American Dream* (New York:

E. P. Dutton and Co., 1948) are somewhat popularized and general. The best on Oliver is Douglas Laing Meikle's dissertation, "James Oliver and the Oliver Chilled Plow Works" (University of Indiana, 1958).

The Northern Indiana Historical Society and the South Bend Public Library have material relating to the city's history. The library has a file of newspaper clippings on South Bend, but it is not indexed or systematically arranged. The greatest disappointment was the failure to find any diaries or unpublished personal accounts of the residents. Only a few brief letters of immigrants were found in the Northern Indiana Historical Society. The most productive sources of information on the life of the urban community were the local newspapers. Approximately a dozen papers appeared and disappeared during the thirty years before 1880, and reminiscences of inhabitants often appeared in later newspapers. The most important are *St. Joseph Valley Register* (1845–84), *National Union* (1866–71), *South Bend Tribune* (weekly—1873–1940), and the *South Bend Daily Tribune* (1873–1940).

The literature on the use of computers and quantitative methodology in history has grown rapidly since 1967, and a full bibliography would fill many pages. A good place to begin, however, would be Robert P. Swierenga, "Computers and American History: The Impact of the 'New' Generation," *Journal of American History* 60 (1974): 1045–70; Theodore K. Rabb, "Guides to Quantitative History: A Review Article," *The Historian* 35 (1973):271–75; or Michael H. Ebner, *The New Urban History: Bibliography on Methodology and Historiography* (Monticello, Ill.: Council of Planning Librarians, 1973). The two best introductions to the use of computers and quantitative methods for the uninitiated historian are Roderick Floud, *An Introduction to Quantitative Methods for Historians* (Princeton: Princeton University Press, 1973), and Edward Shorter, *The Historian and the Computer: A Practical Guide* (Englewood Cliffs, N.J.: Prentice-Hall, Inc., 1971). Earlier comments on the problems historians face when confronted with using a computer are Marshall Smelser and William I. Davison, "The Historian and the Computer: A Simple Introduction to Complex Computation," *Essex Institute Historical Collections* 104 (1968):109–26; Jerome M. Clubb and Howard W. Allen, "Computers and Historical Studies," *Journal of American History* 54 (1967):599–607; and Colin B. Burke, "A Note on Self-teaching, Reference Tools and New Approaches in Quantitative History," *Historical Methods Newsletter* 4 (1971):35–42. The article by Burke contains a good bibliography. There have been several collections of essays that deal with the theoretical and practical problems of a quantitative methodology. Many of these essays attempt to show through example how quantitative methods can be applied to historical research. The best collections are those by William O. Aydelotte, Allan G. Bogue, and Robert William Fogel, eds., *The Dimensions of Quantitative Research in History* (Princeton: Princeton University Press, 1972); Robert P. Swierenga, ed., *Quantification in American History: Theory and Research* (New York: Atheneum, 1970); Don Karl Rowney and James Q. Graham, Jr., eds., *Quantitative History* (Homewood, Ill.: Dorsey Press, 1969); H. J. Dyos, ed., *The Study of Urban History* (New York: St. Martin's Press, 1968), and Edmund A. Bowles, ed., *Computers in Humanistic Research: Readings and Perspectives* (Englewood Cliffs, N.J.: Prentice-Hall, Inc., 1967). An excellent handbook for the historian just beginning to use quantitative methods is Charles M. Dollar and Richard J. Jensen, *Historian's Guide to Statistics: Quantitative Analysis and Historical Research* (New York: Holt, Rinehart and Winston, 1971). The Dollar and Jensen book is more difficult than either of the introductory works by Shorter or Floud, but it contains valuable information on data processing and statistics for historians, as well as an extensive bibliography. For the more advanced, the best guides for the use of statistics in social science research are by Hubert M. Blalock, Jr.: *Social Statistics* (New York: McGraw-Hill, 1960), and *Causal Inferences in Nonexperimental Research* (Chapel Hill: University of North Carolina Press, 1964).

INDEX

Alsace-Lorraine, 137n
Alzey, Hesse-Darmstadt, 105. *See also*
Germany
Andriski, Jacob, 39
Archambeau: family, 53
Assimilation, 107–115, 122
Augsburg, Bavaria, 37

Baden. *See* Germany
Bakanowski, Father Adolph, 57
Barth, Henry, 13–14
Bavarians. *See* Germans
Belgians, 37, 50–51, 61, 67, 78, 89, 95.
See also Other European
Benevolent Aid Association, 27. *See
also* Voluntary associations
Benjamin, Henry, 109
Berthoff, Rowland, 3, 112
Blocked mobility hypothesis, 76, 99,
119–120
Blum, William, 41
Board of Health, 24–25
Booth, Edwin, 108
Boston, 7, 8, 42, 111; Irish in, 55, 83,
87–88
British Americans, 36, 116; leaders of,
102; occupational mobility of, 89;
occupations of, 79, 119; property of,
95; residences of, 52–55, 60, 67
Burns, Arthur, 88
Burr, Frank, 46
Buysse, Edward, 60

Cahill, Henry, 40
Cahill, Hugh, 66
Cahill, John, 66
Canadians. *See* British Americans
Carney, Henry, 40
Catholic Aid Society, 27. *See also*
Voluntary associations
Catholics, 27, 112–113
Census records: use of, 38, 40, 93
Chapin, Horatio, 47
Chicago, 49, 74, 99
Chicago and Lake Huron Railroad Com-
pany, 26. *See also* South Bend: trans-
portation
Chockelt, John, 121
Chudacoff, Howard, 6, 8–9
Citizens National Bank, 71
City. *See* South Bend; Urbanization
Civil War: effect on South Bend's
industries, 75
Classical Institute for French and Ger-
man languages, 28. *See also* South
Bend: schools

Cole, Donald, 8, 9
Colfax, Hest, 51
Colfax, Schuyler, 27, 71, 104, 106
Colmer, Frederick, 121
Coquillard, Alexis, 18–19, 36, 53, 134n
Curti, Merle, 42, 102–103, 107–108.
See also Trempealeau County, Wisconsin

Danes, 51. *See also* Other European
Democrats, 106, 114
Dublin, 53, 55
Dutch, 51. *See also* Other European

Eagle Knitting Company of Elkhart,
143n
Eddy, Colonel Norman, 104
Egbert, Elisha, 27
Elbel's Cornet Band, 109
English, 33–36, 99, 106, 116; leaders of,
102, 106, 111–112, 114–115; occupations of, 79–80, 86–87, 122; persistence
and mobility of, 87, 120; population,
35; property of, 95; residences of, 52,
58, 60, 67. *See also* Great Britain
Ernst, Robert, 7–8, 86
Ethnicity: influence of, on residential
patterns, 48–61, 67–68, 118; influence
of, on leadership, 122–123; and persistence, 43. *See also* Immigrants

First National Bank of South Bend, 75
French, 36, 51–55, 95, 102. *See also*
Other European
French Canadians, 67, 116. *See also*
British Americans
Frenchtown, 60

George, William, 19, 22
German Dramatic Society, 29, 108. *See
also* South Bend: theater
German Select School, 112. *See also*
South Bend: schools
Germania Lodge: Masons, 115. *See also*
Voluntary associations
Germans, 33, 37, 87, 97, 99, 116; leaders
of, 102, 104–115; occupational mobility
of, 83, 86; occupations of, 79, 83–86,
119, 122; persistence of, 120; prejudice
against, 114; property of, 94, 95, 97;
residences of, 53, 56, 58, 60, 67; volun-
tary associations of, 56, 101, 106, 108–
111, 115, 122
Germany, 13, 37, 56, 102, 105
Ginz, Henry, 105–106, 115, 121
Good's Opera House, 29, 108. *See also*
South Bend: theater

153

Goose Pasture, 56, 60
Granger, Father Alexis, 52, 60
Great Britain, 52. *See also* English;
  Scots; Welsh

Haggerty, John, 103
Hanauer, Abram, 85–86
Handlin, Oscar, 6, 7, 86–88, 101, 111
Hanover. *See* Germany
Harris, Robert, 104, 117
Hartwick, Henry, 114
Hesse. *See* Germany
Hoover, Dwight, 4–5
Hose Company Number 1, 110. *See
  also* South Bend: urban services
Hosinski, Frank, 39
Hotels, 45–46
Housing, 45–48, 55, 139n
Hungarians, 36, 51. *See also* Other
  European
Hurd, A. M., 18

Illiteracy, 93. *See also* Schools
Immigrants: birthplace of, 38, 124; index of dissimilarity and segregation
  for, 49–67; intragenerational mobility
  of, 73, 80–89; intergenerational mobility of, 73, 89–93, 120–121; leaders
  of, 100–115, 121–123; occupations
  of, 62–68, 77, 84–90, 92, 99, 125–126;
  persistence of, 42–44, 84–89, 92, 98–
  99; population, 9, 30, 33, 50; property of, 93–99, 127; recruitment of, 32,
  34, 37, 136–137n. *See also names of
  ethnic groups*
Immigration, 3–8, 31–32, 37, 119, 121.
  See also Immigrants
Indiana: immigration to, 35, 39. *See
  also* South Bend
Indiana Reaper and Iron Company,
  142n
Indianapolis, Indiana, 70, 106
Industrialization, 66–68, 74–76; and
  mobility, 91–93, 97–99, 117–120;
  and occupations, 119; and residences,
  67–68, 118. *See also* South Bend; *and
  names of industries*
Irish, 35–36, 83, 116; in Boston, 7–9,
  55, 83, 87–88; geographical mobility
  of, 88; leaders of, 102, 112–113; occupational mobility of, 87–88, 120; occupations of, 53–54, 79, 119; persistence of, 120; property of, 95; residences of, 52–55, 58, 60–61, 67. *See
  also* Great Britain; Immigrants
Italians, 8, 36. *See also* Other Europeans

Klingel, John, 110
Klingel, Philip, 108
Knights, Peter, 5

Knights of Pythias, 110
Knoblock, John C., 65, 70–72, 74, 99,
  106, 121
Knoblock, Otto, 105
Kunstman, Christopher, 94

Ladies Relief Society, 27. *See also*
  South Bend: churches
Lake Shore and Michigan Southern Rail-
  road, 21, 26. *See also* South Bend:
  transportation
Lang, Fred, 114
La Porte County, Indiana, 106
Lawrence, Massachusetts, 8
Leaders, 100–115, 121–123
Lederer, John, 65, 94
Liddisdale, Scotland, 69
Livingston, Moses, 85, 104, 117
Livingston, Myer, 85, 94, 104, 117
Lowell, Indiana, 133n

McNish, David, 41
Maennerchor Society, 110. *See also*
  Germans; Voluntary associations
Mansfield, Ohio, 70
Masons, 28, 101–102, 110, 112, 122.
  See also Voluntary associations
Matthews, George W., 106
Mecklenburg. *See* Germany
Methodists, 27. *See also* South Bend:
  churches
Method: of classification of occupations,
  61–63; of measuring occupational mo-
  bility, 71–73; of measuring residential
  mobility, 49–50. *See also the Preface*
Michigan Central Railroad Company, 26.
  See also South Bend: transportation
Migration patterns, 37–44. *See also*
  Mobility; Immigrants
Miller-Knoblock Electric Company, 105
Milwaukee, 84
Mishawaka, 19, 24, 70, 132–133n
Mobility, 5, 10–12, 31; geographical,
  31–44, 88, 117; industrialization and,
  97–99, 117, 119, 120; intragenerational, 73, 80–89; intergenerational,
  73, 89–93, 120–121; leaders and, 122–
  123; methods for measuring, 49–50,
  61–63, 71–73, 100–102; occupational,
  71–72, 87–93, 99, 119–120; persistence
  and, 42–44, 73, 80, 84–89, 92, 98–99,
  120; residential, 49–67; social, 28, 31,
  71–72. *See also* Immigrants
Morton, Oliver P., 32
Myer, John M., 37

Nelli, Humbert, 8
New Brunswick, 53. *See also* British
  Americans
Newburyport, Massachusetts, 5–6, 8, 10,
  71, 87, 117, 120; property ownership

in, 95–96; South Bend compared to, 81–84. *See also* Thernstrom, Stephan
New York, 52, 84, 86, 88, 106, 111
Northern Indiana College, 28. *See also* South Bend: schools
Nova Scotia, 53. *See also* British Americans

Occupations, 62, 63, 65; classification of, 61–63; and industrialization, 119–121; and mobility, 77–99, 119–120; and property, 95–99; and residences, 49, 51, 60–68; women in, 73. *See also* Immigrants: occupations; South Bend: occupations; *and names of ethnic groups*
Odd Fellows, 28–29, 101, 110, 112, 122. *See also* Voluntary associations
Oliver, James, 10–11, 25, 69, 71, 99, 101, 117, 121; employees of, 66, 79; housing for workers by, 47, 51, 66, 118; inventions by, 70, 75–76; property owned by, 105; recruitment of immigrants by, 32, 34, 37, 136–137n; South Bend Iron Works, 21, 51
Oliver, Joseph, 105
Omaha, 49, 117–118
Other European: occupational mobility of, 89; property owned by, 95; residences of, 50–51, 58, 61. *See also* Immigrants
Out-migration, 132n, 138n. *See also* Mobility

Park, Robert E., 48
Peninsular Railroad Company, 26. *See also* South Bend: transportation
Persistence, 42–44, 73, 80, 103, 120. *See also* Mobility
Philadelphia, 48–49
Poles, 34, 57, 78, 97, 99, 117–119; leaders of, 102, 106–107, 113–114, 123; migration patterns of, 39; occupational mobility of, 89, 119–120; in politics, 106–107, 113; residences of, 57–58, 60–61, 68, 113, 118; social mobility of, 115; voluntary associations of, 113–115, 123
Police, 22–23
Polish Prussia, 34, 117–118. *See also* Germany, Poles
Poughkeepsie, New York, 84, 96
Prejudice, 108–109, 113–115
Property, 93–99, 104–105, 127. *See also* Immigrants; South Bend
Prussia: leaders, 102. *See also* Germans, Germany

Radatski, Charles, 60
Real estate. *See* Property
Rennoe, Joseph, 38

Republicans, 106
Residences: boarders in, 45–47; ethnicity and, 50–61, 68, 118; housing density, 47–48, 139n; of immigrants, 45–46; industrialization and, 54–55, 63–68; of leaders, 104; methods of measuring patterns of, 49–50; and mobility, 55–56; and occupations, 61–68; patterns of, 48–68. *See also* Immigrants; Mobility; South Bend
Rockstroh, Kasper, 71, 94
Ross, Benjamin, 27
Russworm, Andrew, 94

Sack, John, 25
Saint Casimir Society, 113
Saint Joseph County, 63, 74
Saint Joseph County Savings Bank, 71
Saint Joseph County Total Abstinence Society, 27
Saint Joseph Hotel, 45
Saint Joseph Medical Society, 25
Saint Joseph Reaper and Machine Company, 142n
Saint Joseph River, 74
Saint Joseph's Academy, 28. *See also* South Bend: schools
Saint Joseph's Catholic Church, 24, 52–54
Saint Joseph's Catholic Church (Polish), 57
Saint Patrick's Church, 53–54, 112–113
Saint Patrick's Grammar School, 28. *See also* South Bend: schools
Saint Stanislaus Kostka Society, 113–115
Saxony. *See* Germany
Schlesinger, Arthur, Sr., 4
Schools, 27–28, 105
Scots, 87, 102, 112. *See also* Great Britain
Segregation. *See* Residences
Seneca County, New York, 69–70
Shively's Hall, 108
Singer Sewing Machine Company, 11, 20–21, 62, 75–76, 117, 121
Skelly, Lawrence, 60
Social mobility, 28, 71–72. *See also* Blocked mobility hypothesis, Immigrants; Mobility; Occupations; Residences
Social organizations, 108–115, 122–123
Social Sciences Methodology, 4–5. *See also* Method
Sorinsville, 53–54
South Bend: business growth of, 20, 22, 73–74; churches, 27–28; compared to Newburyport, 82, 83; crime, 22–23, 70; early growth of, 13–22, 116–117; housing in, 45–48, 55, 139n; industrialization of, 20–21, 66–68, 74–76, 91–93, 97–99, 116–119; justification for

study of, 9–12; occupations in, 77,
90, 96, 125–126; population in, 9,
19, 30, 33, 50, 54, 124, 133n; property in, 93–99, 127; schools in, 27–
28, 105; social life in, 26–29, 108–
115; theater in, 29, 108; transporta-
tion in, 18, 21, 25–26, 55; urban
services in, 10, 22–26
South Bend Chilled Plow Company, 71,
142n. *See also* John C. Knoblock
South Bend Gas Light Company, 23.
See also South Bend: urban services
South Bend Hydraulic Company, 75.
See also South Bend: industrialization
South Bend Iron Works, 21, 69–70.
See also James Oliver
South Bend Union Relief Association,
27. *See also* South Bend: churches
South Bend Street Railway, 26.
See also South Bend: urban services
Spencerian Commercial College, 28.
See also South Bend: schools
Sports, 109
Srole, Leo, 6
Staley, A. C. and Sons, 75. *See also*
South Bend: industrialization
Stanfield, Judge William, 106
Still, Bayrd, 9
Studebaker Brothers Manufacturing
Company, 10–11, 20–21, 66, 68, 75–
76, 79, 117, 121; housing for workers
by, 47, 66, 118; recruiting of immi-
grants by, 32, 34, 37, 136–137n. *See
also* South Bend: industrialization
Studebaker, John M., 104
Swedes, 36, 50–51, 78; occupational
mobility of, 89; property of, 95;
residences of, 51, 61. *See also* Other
European
Swiss, 36, 50–51. *See also* Other
European

Tanski, Nicholas, 102, 106, 113
Telephone Exchange Company, 25.
See also South Bend: urban services
Theater, 29, 108. *See also* South Bend:
social life

Thernstrom, Stephan: *Poverty and
Progress,* 5–6, 8, 11, 117; mobility,
71, 81–83; occupations, 61, 76
Transportation, 18, 21, 25–26, 55.
See also South Bend: urban services
Trempealeau County, Wisconsin, 42,
102–103, 107–108, 111
Turner, Frederick Jackson, 42
Turnock, Edwin, 53
Turnverein, 56, 101, 106, 108–111,
115, 122. *See also* Germans

Urbanization, 3–4, 116–117; definition
of, 9; ethnicity and, 3–10, 30–31, 55,
118; growth of urban services and, 22–
26; historical interpretations of, 4–9;
immigration and, 3, 5–12, 30–31, 67–
68, 76, 91, 99, 117–121; industrialization and, 3, 6–8, 10–11, 21–22, 63, 67–
68, 76, 117–121; mobility and, 3–9,
11–12, 30–31, 121; occupational mobility and, 4, 6–8, 10–12, 31, 71, 91,
119–120; as a process, 4–5, 8–9, 11–12,
30–31, 117–118. *See also* South Bend
Unemployment, 93
University of Notre Dame, 28, 53, 61
Urban services, 10, 22–26, 55

Van Vennett, 37, 41
Voluntary associations, 24, 28–29,
108–115, 122–123

Wages, 63, 74, 78
Wales. *See* Great Britain
Wapello County, Iowa, 42
Ward, David, 6
Warden, Joseph, 105
Warner, Sam B., Jr., 10, 48–49
Warner, W. Lloyd, 6
Weber, Adna, 6, 39
Welsh, 87. *See also* Great Britain
Wittke, Carl, 3, 34
Württemberg, 56. *See also* Germany

Young Hoosier Company, 24. *See also*
Voluntary associations; South Bend:
urban services